Wealthy U:

Seven Sacred Wealth & Wisdom Lessons

by Marilyn August

HappyAbout.info

20660 Stevens Creek Blvd., Suite 210
Cupertino, CA 95014

First Printing: March 2008
Paperback ISBN: 978-1-60005-099-2
Place of Publication: Silicon Valley, California, U.S.
Paperback Library of Congress Number: 2008923805

eBook ISBN: 987-160005-100-5

Trademarks

Warning and Disclaimer

Praise for 'Wealthy U'

"A must read for commissioned sales people and business owners. Marilyn August challenges embedded money myths most of us have with her seven lessons that power through yours and your prospect's limiting beliefs about money. Her ideas and concepts promise that you will close more deals for more money once you incorporate Marilyn's money philosophy into your professional life. Works as well for personal money relationships as couples learn how to think differently about money."

J. Scott Bailey, Owner,
Sandler Regional Training Center, Irvine, CA

"An inspiring, unique look at the "psychology" of money, Wealthy U encourages readers to think about money and success in a different way. Ms. August's lessons and "wallet wisdom" are insightful, creative and eye-opening. Using real-life examples, Ms. August guides readers through the steps required to achieve true wealth and wisdom. Highly recommended!"

Deanna Brown, Attorney-at-Law,
Senior Corporate Counsel,
Skyworks Solutions, Irvine, CA

"Marilyn, you have a gift for getting people to think differently about money. That new outlook really opened up doors for me. In fact, I added an anchor client that more than doubled what I make on a monthly basis. I have accomplished more in the past three months than I have in the past year. Thanks to you I have a better understanding that money is just energy, a symbol of appreciation that others give me and I pass along."

Henry DeVries, New Client Marketing Institute,
San Diego, CA

Author

- Marilyn August
  http://wealthyu.com

Publisher

- Mitchell Levy
  http://happyabout.info

Production

- Monica Valdez
  http://publishing-consultants.com

Cover Design

- Cate Calson
  http://calsongraphics.com

Dedication

This book is dedicated to the
Loving Memory of my Mother and Father,
Helen and Joseph Greenberger.
Immigrants to the United States, you cherished this country
and
the opportunities it offered your children.
May you both rest in peace!
AND...

To the thousands of *Wealth and Wisdom Seminar* participants
as well as to my coaching clients,
all who have had the courage to take their
personal journey to wealth and wisdom.
This book is dedicated to fulfilling your dream of living a
joyously prosperous life.

Acknowledgements

I wish to thank my teachers and mentors—who are too numerous to name—and a special thank you to three people who have been there for me over the years:

Susan Velasquez, author of Beyond Intellect: Journey into the Wisdom of Your Intuition, and founder of the ongoing "Unleash the Power of Your Intuition" seminars.

Henry DeVries, co-author of Client Seduction: Step-by-Step Lead Generation System for Professional and Technology Service Firms, and founder of the New Client Marketing Institute, without whom this book would not have been finished.

Michael Whelan, D.C., of the Vitalistic Healing Center in Laguna Hills, California, for his commitment to healing mind, body, and spirit.

A Message from Happy About®

Thank you for your purchase of this Happy About book. It is available online at http://happyabout.info/wealthyu.php or at other online and physical bookstores.

- Please contact us for quantity discounts at sales@happyabout.info
- If you want to be informed by e-mail of upcoming Happy About® books, please e-mail bookupdate@happyabout.info

Happy About is interested if you are an author who would like to submit a non-fiction book proposal or a corporation that would like to have a book written for you. Please contact us by e-mail at editorial@happyabout.info or by phone at 1-408-257-3000.

Other Happy About books available include:

- I'm on LinkedIn -- Now What???
  http://happyabout.info/linkedinhelp.php
- Happy About Online Networking:
  http://happyabout.info/onlinenetworking.php
- Tales From the Networking Community:
  http://happyabout.info/networking-community.php
- Happy About Being a Baby Boomer:
  http://happyabout.info/babyboomer/newfound-longevity.php
- Scrappy Project Management:
  http://happyabout.info/scrappyabout/project-management.php
- 42 Rules of Marketing
  http://happyabout.info/42rules/marketing.php
- Foolosophy:
  http://happyabout.info/foolosophy.php
- The Home Run Hitter's Guide to Fundraising:
  http://happyabout.info/homerun-fundraising.php
- Confessions of a Resilient Entrepreneur:
  http://happyabout.info/confessions-entrepreneur.php
- Memoirs of the Money Lady:
  http://happyabout.info/memoirs-money-lady.php
- Happy About Tax Relief: The Offer in Compromise Solution
  http://happyabout.info/oic.php
- Rule #1: Stop Talking! A Guide to Listening
  http://happyabout.info/listenerspress/stoptalking.php
- Communicating the American Way
  http://happyabout.info/communicating-american-way.php

"The money did not physically exist. Even "real" money was only specially made paper printed with black ink on the front and green on the back. What backed the money was not gold or something of intrinsic value, but rather the collective belief that money had value because it had to have such value. Thus it was that the monetary system of the United States and every other country in the world was an exercise in psychology, a thing of the mind."

Tom Clancy, <u>Debt of Honor</u>

Contents

Preface

Before I Started My Own Journey...

to wealth and wisdom, money was a serious problem for me. I had many good corporate jobs, and to the outsider I'm sure I appeared to be doing just fine, but nobody could ever have imagined that the lack of money was like a giant monster controlling me. I constantly lived in fear of not having enough, but at the same time I overspent, running up significant debt on my credit cards. I treated myself as if I were nothing more than a bank account, judging my self-worth by how much money I had on any given day—lots of money meant I was a good person, while a skinny bank balance told me I was worthless. My money problems became the secret black cloud hanging over my head, keeping me awake at night and following me everywhere. And it seemed like no one else had this demon running their life.

Without being fully aware, I was allowing my fears to limit my income, simply by staying in jobs where I was unhappy and did not seem to "fit."

My natural ability—to find clarity through the muck and focus energy to create results—was definitely not welcomed in these environments. I repeatedly found myself in miserable personal and professional situations. I have been both fired and laid off from jobs where I knew I was capable and competent—if only someone would listen to me. I was a passive victim without even knowing it.

It followed that no matter what I did to survive, I never seemed to have enough money. The bottom line was that I felt inadequate and stupid more often than anything else. At that point in my life, I had not made the connection between my attitude about myself and the amount of money I had, or how I used or abused that money. I was just one of many people who believed that if only I won the lottery, all my problems would be solved, I would finally have enough money, and my life would be great forever after.

My dark money secret continued to slowly eat away at my self-respect. Finally, I hit the bottom and knew that I had to find solutions to my money dilemma. I turned to reading and researching to find answers. The few books available at the time did not make sense to me. There was nowhere to look, except deeper within myself. Thus began my inner journey to the depths of my soul. There, inside of me, I found that *I* was the core of my money problems, exposing negative money beliefs buried deep in my subconscious. As these hidden beliefs surfaced, I began developing new ways of thinking about money, as well as tools and techniques for changing my financial behaviors.

Almost without design, I found my passion for helping others on their journey to wealth and wisdom. My own pain and struggle with money motivated me to combine my professional background as a corporate trainer with my personal experiences, and in 1990 I founded Wealth and Wisdom Seminars, a company dedicated to transforming your personal relationship with money and by extension, your relationship with yourself and your self-worth. Through my seminar program, thousands of people have changed their relationship to money, which in turn has led them to have prosperous, peaceful, and more productive and purposeful lives.

I invite you to use this book as a guide to your personal Wealthy U.

Sorry, No Fast Food Fix

In a world of instant gratification and more than a few "millionaire-in-a-minute" books, it is somewhat nervy to suggest that attaining both wealth and wisdom is a journey. The problem with the fast food fix approach is that, like a meal eaten too fast, it provides only a temporary high. Wealth, or the lack of it, really is a window into your soul. Think of wealth as a metaphor for how you are living your life: fearful or fearless, risk taker or security first, committed to breakthrough or satisfied to drift through life never quite fulfilled or joyous. Money, or the lack of it, is an outward mirroring of your cherished and often mistaken beliefs about life, money, and your relationship to money, as well as your place in the world. Creating sustained wealth and the wisdom to use it well is first and foremost an internal journey into the very depths of your soul. This journey tunnels into your value system, opens up more flexible emotional boundaries, increases clarity, focus, and direction—resulting in living the life you love.

The Journey to Wealth and Wisdom includes gaining a deeper internal knowledge of who you are and learning to trust yourself. Second guessing and regrets tend to disappear and are replaced with clarity of purpose, passion, and money. You are less likely to be pulled off course into old ways of thinking about money.

You will notice that some fine and subtle distinctions are being made on this complex, yet direct journey to wealth and wisdom. One of these distinctions is between greed and true wealth. Greed is simply the desire to satisfy some unconscious need to buy self-esteem, status, or love, while true wealth is the kind of prosperity that sustains over time, with more than enough money to fuel your richly fulfilled life.

A truly "wealthy" relationship with your finances means that money is simply the engine that drives the dream machine. It is the energy powering your dreams, without which, it is rather difficult to accomplish a higher degree of functioning in the world. Wisdom includes the ethics, morality and generosity of spirit with which money is generated, stewarded, and spent. Including wisdom with wealth answers the unspoken vexing question, "How come so many apparently wealthy people can have so much money and be so miserable?"

Have you ever wondered why some people who seem to have great wealth are so tight with it or why others constantly worry about losing it? Have you pondered the debts of lottery winners and the financially destructive behaviors of celebrities?

The reasons are obviously complex, more so than simply saying that there is more to wealth than having lots of money. Internal self-awareness and wisdom are part of the answer to what builds and sustains wealth without the dysfunction often associated with it. Wisdom is the ability to be conscious of emotional trigger points, make accurate observations about a particular situation, and then have the courage to make new, more positive choices. When woven together, wealth and wisdom nourish a life worth living to its richest and fullest.

You may be one of those people who have been sold on the idea of better money management as the simplistic answer to any money dilemma. If you could only figure out just how to budget correctly, or better yet, magically read the future. If only you knew where the stock market is going or if a business decision made today is guaranteed to generate additional revenues tomorrow. The perfect budget, sticking to it religiously, investing properly, and still feeling fearful about having enough money does not make for a fulfilling life. Money is more than simple math and numbers. Emotion, beliefs, and preconceived notions are all tied up with it because money is associated with not only survival, but beyond survival to thriving. The answer to money problems lies more in managing *yourself* in relationship to the money you have now.

~~~~~~~~~~~~~

Wallet Wisdom Lesson

You cannot manage money.
You can only manage yourself,
your relationship to the money you have,
and the money you desire.

~~~~~~~~~~~~~

Money is an Agreement

Money is an idea, a concept, and a collective agreement holding that particular pieces of paper and round metal coins have a specific value. It is universally agreed that the number one (1) with lots of zeros (0000) after it, printed on special paper, has more value than the number one with no zeros printed after it. You can travel the world, and while the colors might change and exchange rates differ, money in whatever color and denomination is the agreed means of exchange. Money is exchanged an an agreement of value; value given for value received. The only thing that you can actually do with money is to trade it for something you value. You may save it or invest it, but eventually, you will circulate it as a means of exchange or give it away for some noble purpose.

The simplicity of the universally accepted value agreement may be logical, but the emotions attached to money are anything but logical. At its core, money is perceived as the very means of survival. This alone triggers the desire to obtain more money. It also triggers the fear of loss, fear of being ripped off, fear of misusing, and toss in anger at past mistakes for good measure. It becomes more obvious that the journey on which you are about to embark is more complex than a "fast food" temporary fix; it is a journey toward eliminating stress and worry about money, and replacing them with much more money. The journey will change how you relate emotionally, spiritually, and intellectually to your self-worth, and by extension, will lead you to better managing the money you have and the money you want.

Your relationship to money is first and foremost an extension of your mental relationship to yourself. It is a thing of the mind. Your mind is a very powerful computer; it imprints information from the past, and beyond your personal past to that of your parents and grandparents and beyond. The mind is like an iceberg with its bulk hidden under the water; only part of what is stored in the mind is known, or conscious. Most negative attitudes and behaviors about money are stored in the part of the mind called the subconscious, which is below the surface of self-awareness. Being "unconscious" is the opposite of being self-aware, and, like an iceberg, this state of mind creates havoc with that which cannot be seen. Until you are consciously aware of the beliefs stored in your unconscious mind, there is little you can do to change them. As Albert Einstein said, "*you cannot solve a problem at the same level of consciousness that created it.*"

This concept is easier to understand if you imagine that you are walking along the street and find $20 just lying on the sidewalk. It doesn't appear to belong to anyone, and it is fair to assume that it was dropped and forgotten. As you reach down to pick it up, a small voice in your head says "*Don't pick up that dirty money.*" You hesitate and decide that you had better not touch the money. It might have germs on it or bring back luck. The unconscious negative conclusion you reached in an instant may have been that *money has to be hard to come by* or something similar. The important part is not the $20 or whether you accept it, but the awareness that you may unconsciously push money away from you if it comes too easily. Once aware of this response, you can make a new choice and change your attitudes to receiving money easily and with gratitude.

The Seven Sacred Lessons

The path to wealth and wisdom does not always follow a straight line. Think about an airplane that is flying a non-stop to its destination. It may still be subject to wind patterns that push it off course. The pilot's job is to constantly make course corrections so the plane lands at its intended destination. You may experience times when you fly to your destination of wealth with ease, but you also may encounter turbulence. At times, there will be forks in the road, requiring you to make a financial decision that may feel off course at the time, but it really is just part of the journey. Sometimes the prosperity road will be unimpeded and wide, while at other times you may have to maneuver more carefully because obstacles lie in your way. You are the pilot of your personal wealth and wisdom. The Seven Sacred Lessons are agreements you make with yourself. They are like a personal navigation system to help you make appropriate, conscious course corrections on your journey to wealth.

Simply put, you cannot get to where you are going if you do not know where you are. Remember, money is an inanimate object. It may be surprising to discover that you cannot manage money, you can only manage yourself in relationship to money. Managing yourself includes managing your beliefs and attitudes toward money, paying attention to details, nurturing and respecting your money as you respect yourself, and most importantly, relating to money simply as a tool to support a fulfilled, purposeful lifestyle.

~~~~~~~~~~~~~~

Wallet Wisdom Lesson

Money is a teacher~
It teaches you about yourself,
your values, and how you operate your life.
Money opens a window into your Soul.

~~~~~~~~~~~~~~

Mile markers along the journey to wealth and wisdom include insights; those moments of self-awareness and new behavior changes. Even relatively small changes are cause for celebration. For example, something as simple as asking more questions than usual before making a financial decision is cause for celebration. Saying "no" to something you instinctively know is not in your best interests is reason enough to give yourself a verbal "yea!" Small changes lead to bigger, more powerful changes. Celebrate the wins without judging them as big or small.

The Seven Sacred Lesson Agreements are guaranteed to churn up and expose deeply hidden negative and self-defeating beliefs about money, prosperity, and being wealthy, as well as unconscious fears of having too much money. The word "agree" is defined in part as *become or be in harmony*, while "agreement" is defined as *to consent or agree*. The Seven Sacred Lesson agreements are a contract you make with yourself to commit to the 36 prosperity lessons. When you make a commitment to keep these agreements, you will notice an almost immediate change in how you relate to money. If you keep them near to your heart, these agreements will accelerate the rate of achieving your dreams, helping you cut down the amount of time you spend on dead-end pursuits, and assisting you in determining the best choices for your situation.

Breakthroughs happen more easily, effortlessly, and much quicker than in the past when using lessons as guideposts on your wealth and wisdom journey. They propel you to move outside your self-imposed limitations and to focus on changing your mindset from non-productive behavior to positive, prosperous action. They bring along with them new behavior and a deeper consciousness of your financial patterns and behaviors. Awareness is the magic potion of true wealth and wisdom. It is nearly impossible to be truly wealthy unless you know what prosperous changes will work to your best interest.

The Seven Sacred Lesson agreements include:

1. **Stop complaining, blaming, and worrying about money:** "Complaining and blaming" could be defined as ruminating on the past and being a victim to past circumstances about which you can do nothing. Closely related to complaining and blaming, worry is a fear of what is to come and implies the need to control your future. Money is not generated in the past or in the future, it is generated in the present. Spending your emotional time and creative energy complaining, blaming, and worrying are actually draining energy that you could use to generate money.
2. **Be creative, open, and flexible to generating and receiving money:** Most people have blinders on when considering their options for generating and receiving money. Refusing to change the way you think about money—about how it is generated or received—can limit you in some very significant ways. Negative beliefs, judgments, and assumptions can erect a mental cage around wealth and wisdom.
3. **Be current and complete on all financial transactions:** Stay up-to-date and pay attention to details regarding your money, such as opening and paying bills in a timely manner. Balance your checkbooks and keep your financial house in order. Unresolved financial matters are like carrying around a ball and chain from the past, and avoidance and denial only make matters worse. Resolving dysfunctional money issues clears the way for

you to increase your income. As you begin to take care of money details and steward the money you currently possess, you might be surprised at how easy it is to consider yourself capable of handling larger amounts of money.

4. **Think before I buy or do not spend at all:** Comfort shopping will only give you a temporary "high." Compulsive, impulsive spending usually leads to regret, giving the subconscious mind a powerful, negative message that you are not capable of having more than enough money—because you will somehow blow it. On a typical day, you will be bombarded with approximately 10,000 commercial messages that encourage you to "Buy, buy, buy!" Be a conscious consumer by doing whatever necessary to give yourself a moment to think before making any purchase.

5. **Communicate openly and honestly with myself and others:** Money is one of our last taboos, which makes honest communication about it extremely difficult. It is a highly charged, emotional subject that is especially explosive among families. Many people would rather get themselves into money stress than to tell the financial truth to themselves or to others. Willingness to speak the truth with kindness, dignity, and respect for yourself and others makes money discussions safe and productive.

6. **Trust myself to make reasonable and rational financial decisions:** Because you cannot foretell the future, you sometimes must make financial decisions with inadequate information. Most people make the best decisions they can with the information they have available. Take time to evaluate, consider, and trust yourself and *then* take the next step. Trust your own processes and be gentle with yourself. As you gain confidence and trust yourself, it becomes safe to acquire the money you desire.

7. **Take appropriate action when breaking these agreements:** There may be times when you forget about or when you have not paid attention to one or several of these Agreements. Take the necessary action to get back into alignment with them. When you use these Agreements as valuable learning tools, they have the ability to guide and direct you to wealth and wisdom.

Please note the suggested Action Items at the end of some chapters. These action items are self-awareness exercises; there is not one right or wrong answer to any of the questions. Rather, the purpose of each Action Item is to become more conscious (self-aware) of your financial behaviors so you can make the appropriate changes. It is impossible to change or to access wealth until you are conscious of the attitudes, behaviors, and hidden beliefs that keep you stuck.

Chapter

1 Don't Worry, Be Happy

I agree to stop complaining, blaming, and worrying about money.

Complaining, blaming, and worrying about money are nothing more than victim behaviors that focus on the past or the fearful future rather than on generating more money. These mental ruminations are actually passive, non-productive behaviors that stunt your possibilities for generating money. Closely related, these three reactions to money tend to spill over into one another. Worrying often leads to complaining, and if you are in the complainer mode, you often begin looking for someone to blame for your money dilemmas. Whether you find yourself engaging in one or more of these behaviors, they leave little room for creative, positive, and productive thoughts and actions.

While worrying, complaining, and blaming are destructive and are the opposite of taking effective action, worrying is perhaps the most common of these behaviors. Many people are so accustomed to worrying about money that they never seem to talk about one without the other—money and worry seem married to each other. Ironically, worrying about money seems to repel money instead of drawing it to you. How worry repels money cannot be explained logically, especially to the person who is so accustomed to it that they wouldn't know what to do without their gloom and doom mode of conversation. But think about the last time you were worried about money—did you generate more money? Wait! There was a young woman who managed to manipulate her father into giving her some money by constantly having a "woe is me I am so worried" conversation with him. Her dad fed her victim habit, rather than ignoring her constant complaining or addressing her problem by forcing her to take responsibility for her finances. However, his quick fix did not solve her money problems; her worry was actually repelling money rather than attracting it.

A professional sales person knows better than most and understands what happens when they are focused only on making the sale or on how much money they will make. The person knows that focusing on the money rather than the customers will be a fast way to lose the sale, in the end. The transference of money through sales doesn't just happen, although it seems random and beyond logic. In reality, it is anything but random since worry is more akin to failure than to success. Money is pushed away. The same thing seems to happen when you are desperate and worried about a check arriving on time; somehow it always seems to be delayed. The worry is actually creating a negative energy field around your very being that gives you more worry, but not more money.

~~~~~~~~~~~~~

Wallet Wisdom Lesson

Worry is like a rocking chair;
it gives you something to do but
gets you nowhere.

~~~~~~~~~~~~~

Worrying about money is a habit you may have learned by example from family or friends or as a result of poor decision-making, but it is one you can change by recognizing when you worry and how it affects your behavior as well as your wealth. The act of worrying is nothing more a deep fear about the future and a feeling of panic about not being able to control it. People who habitually worry that the future will be bleak have a wonderful excuse to do nothing to change that future. Such people willingly remain a victim to circumstances they perceive as being beyond their control, rather than attempting to break out of the rut and take control. Giving up worry is not the same thing as denying present circumstances, nor is it an excuse to act irresponsibly with money. There may be some valid reason for an immediate concern, and that concern drives productive action; therefore, you can make a distinction between when you are paying attention to your true needs in the present and when you are giving valuable time to unnecessary worries. Worry is a mental exercise that includes analysis without coming to a solution, bending the ear of those around you with your tale of woe, or throwing up your hands and refusing to handle the situation because you are fearful.

Action Item—The Worry Log

The Worry Log is a powerful tool to help you break the worry habit. A Worry Log is one of those actions steps that may not seem to make sense until you realize how much time and energy you spend worrying about money. Ceasing the worry habit is much easier when you are consciously aware of the real costs of such worry to your physical, emotional, and financial health.

The Worry Log is for the chronic worrier or even the unconscious worrier. It is meant to help them initially manage their worry, and then eventually break the worry habit. This self-analysis tool requires some time and effort, but becomes a visible measurement of the ways in which your worry habit controls you and is well worth the time.

A Worry Log consists of pages of a notebook pad divided into three columns. Head each column with the following labels: *Date*, *Event*, and *Time*. When you catch yourself worrying about money, take the time to record it.

A WORRY LOG

Date	Event	Time

After maintaining your Worry Log for a few days, it will be easy to identify repeating patterns. Analyzing these worry patterns will help you find ways to use your time more productively. Are there certain events or times of day that cause you to worry more than others? You may find that you worry more when you are alone or on the drive home from work with nothing else to occupy your mind.

You will probably tire of keeping a Worry Log within a week or so, but that is exactly the point of filling out the log. You will see with your own eyes just how wasteful it is to spend your precious mind time worrying. Why waste time worrying when you can be more creative about generating money? Once you realize what is financially threatening, you can begin replacing your worry habit with effective action. Take control, for example, by mentally disciplining yourself to stay in the moment—thinking positively about what you already have instead of what is missing. It may be as simple as asking yourself, "Do I have enough money for today?" or "Is there food in the house and gas in the car?" Stay present by saying to yourself or writing in your own handwriting, "I have enough money for what I need today," or "I am safe and protected right now." By turning your thoughts to what you have instead of what you fear is unobtainable, you will create an affirming, positive, and present mind set.

~~~~~~~~~~~~~

Wallet Wisdom Lesson

Money cannot
penetrate a
wall of fear.

~~~~~~~~~~~~~

Just as worry will not generate money, neither will complaining and blaming. It is just as destructive to your journey to wealth and wisdom to complain and blame as it is to worry, nor is such behavior any more effective at increasing your income. Complaining that someone or something other than you must be at fault for your lousy predicament does not produce money. While you may get momentary comfort by casting blame on others, in reality you simply have found a way to avoid taking responsibility for your finances. Unfortunately, with this attitude, you remain a victim of past as well as current circumstances. Victims, by definition, are powerless to change or improve their lot in life. In this sense, when you remain the victim, you recreate the very thing you don't want: a lack of money. You have the same internal power to take control and make the necessary changes as the young man below who changed his complaining habit into a well-paying job.

Jordan wondered, "Why do I spend so much money on computer games? They bore me after a few days, and I go out and buy more, even when I haven't paid all my bills." In order to help him understand the answer to his question, he needed to look deeper for the reason he purchased computer games. When he took some time to reflect on his job, he realized that it failed to challenge him. Upon further thought, he discovered that the computer games served as a substitute for the challenges his employment failed to provide him. Once he understood the true cause of his complaint, he began to think about how he could better use his time and money by looking for a more fulfilling job.

Even while he celebrated this insight, he complained, "I don't have a college education." This bright, capable man acted the part of a victim by deciding that he simply could not get a better job without a college education. Jordan had an important choice to make. He could live the rest of his life complaining about the lack of a college education and blaming circumstances for his spending habits, or he could take action.

After an ongoing dialogue and some encouragement, he decided to take action and send out resumes on what he thought might be a small chance that he could improve his employment situation. He was pleasantly surprised to find a job that gave him the opportunity to use natural computer skills and talents. His employer was so pleased with Jordan's abilities to solve problems that he agreed to provide tuition assistance if Jordan would agree to stay with the company for a set period of time after finishing school. In addition to finding a great job and a supportive boss, Jordan's salary was considerably higher than he had been receiving at his previous position. Had he continued complaining and playing the part of a victim, Jordan would not have gotten into more comfortable financial circumstances, nor would he have found a new and more challenging job or the opportunity to go to college.

Even people who have large amounts of money can find themselves locked in the complainer-victim mode. From the outside, Charlie seemed to have it all—two homes, one at the beach and the other a grand country estate. The time and leisure to entertain friends and fly his own plane, and the opportunity to sell luxury cars as a hobby. Even while living what seemed to be an idyllic life, Charlie still found cause for complaint. Nothing gave him joy or pleasure; instead, he expressed disdain for almost everything. One bland day blended into another. His life consisted of a series of meaningless events. Even a trip to Europe or his nights out with friends were no longer enjoyable. He might as well have been homeless for all the stress and angst that were his constant companions. The hole in his soul seemed beyond repair; he had no vision for living a purposeful, fulfilled life. Sadly, even while he appeared to have everything, he had nothing because he appreciated none of what he had.

~~~~~~~~~~~~~

Wallet Wisdom Lesson

There is not enough money in the world
to fill a
hole in the soul!

~~~~~~~~~~~~~

Even if you are not specifically complaining about money, sometimes money is at the root of the complaint. John was worried about finding the right woman with whom to settle down and have a family. In large part, his worry was due to the fact that he didn't think he had enough money to attract the woman of his dreams. This self-defeating belief combined with his complaint that he was just "unlucky in love," would definitely keep him single for a long time.

Both John and Charlie would rather complain than do anything to change their situation. They both send out negative energy, focusing on what was "missing" from their lives rather than on the multitude of things that were available. They were very convincing and, in a perverse way, seemed to be enjoying themselves as they spun their sad tales of woe. Taking positive action steps has the power to break the complaining cycle, and at the same time, relieve those around them from hearing the same "poor me" conversation.

Notice the lack of action and limitations in the mental exercise of the complainer, blamer, and worry modes. It is practically impossible to complain, blame, and worry when you are in motion toward your desired wealth. Sometimes you may not know the exact action step to take in order to break these behaviors. The action you take does not necessarily have to make sense at the time. For example, if you are worrying about paying the bills on time, you may want to get everything ready to pay them, such as write the checks and put stamps on the envelopes, even before you have the money to actually mail the payments. Even if you do not necessarily want to change jobs or start your own business, you can read the classified ads or check the Internet regularly for new opportunities to increase your income.

One powerful Action Item is to make a list of the required and negotiable characteristics of your ideal job or business, as Judy did. She had a two-hour commute to work each day. Judy loved her job, but she constantly complained about the long drive that sapped her energy, and worried about the cost of gas for her daily commute. Instead of giving up and doing nothing, she went into action, designing her ideal job on paper before she even started looking for a job.

She made a list of requirements:

1. No more than a 45-minute drive from home.
2. Comprehensive medical coverage for me and my family.
3. Interesting, challenging work.

4. Ability to use my creativity and to advance in the company.
5. Stable, consistent income with a generous commission or a pay-for-performance bonus plan.

Notice that Judy did not name the exact job, company, or location; rather, she got clear about her particular job requirements. The very act of writing down what she wanted instead of worrying about the outcome created more options and clarity of thought. For her and for you, the list could be much longer and would most likely change and be refined as the job search progressed. What matters is that she took the time to refocus her energy, concentrating on what she wanted instead of complaining about what she had.

Once Judy had made her list, she updated her resume and brought it to a professional for review. Judy moved beyond the confines of her current job dilemma, opened her mind, and committed to taking action without knowing exactly how the ideal job would find her. Judy trusted herself to move forward without worrying about the outcome. Before long, Judy was offered a job at double her current income for a company located closer to her home.

The ideal customer/client profile works equally well for business owners. Business owners are particularly prone to falling into the complainer and worry mode, especially when they worry about having enough customers, making payroll, or paying their other obligations on time. Instead of the *woe is me* self-talk, having a strong understanding of who they want to do business with and why works like magic in attracting the right client base and increasing revenues. Worry, complaining, and blaming do not generate money—regardless of your circumstances or profession or income level.

You have within you the power to break the cycle of worrying, complaining, and blaming. Learn to live in the paradox of staying present (which is the opposite of complaining, blaming and worrying!) and, simultaneously, take some time to ponder your prosperous future. Athletes know and use the power of the future mindset all the time to win their competitions. They do not worry about what might happen in the future or ruminate about the last lost game other than to learn from their mistakes. You often hear powerful athletes speak about being focused on the outcome rather than the process. While they are no doubt skilled and practiced in the techniques of their sport, they also must believe strongly in their ability to win. You have probably heard Olympic champions talk about how they "see the gold medal around their necks" or how they just "knew" they would capture the win this time.

~~~~~~~~~~~~~~

Wallet Wisdom Lesson

Pain pushes, vision pulls.

~~~~~~~~~~~~~~

Coaches often encourage their players to visualize themselves winning the game before it even starts. In the same way that athletes visualize winning the game, envisioning your wealth and wisdom is equally powerful. Knowing what you want is more important than worrying about how to achieve it. Many great teachers have voiced this same principle; Stephen R. Covey[1] says "start with the end in mind." Now is the time to put this powerful principle into motion by creating a personal global vision statement. Doing this exercise automatically reduces worry, complaining, and blaming because you have moved beyond your current problems, giving your mind a new focus.

A vision statement also helps you to decide how you will use money, what you will buy with it, and what is not important before you even have the money you are thinking about. As you create your vision statement, think of yourself as a painter or a novelist writing the story of your richly fulfilled life just as you envision it. Use broad-brush strokes or overview sentences. Unlike finding the right job or clients, creating a vision statement is a broader view of the rich lifestyle you desire. For example, if you long for a home on the beach, you would make the statement, "I own a beach house" in the present tense. Describing the details of the house you desire or your plan for attaining this house will come later. Think of your vision as a dream that you have no idea how to accomplish right now.

Because your desires can seem to reside so far in the distant future or perhaps they seem difficult to attain at all, some people may resist writing their personal vision statement. Financial upset and drama may be so familiar that it is difficult to think outside of your current problems. This reaction is somewhat uncommon, but the only thing to do with

1. Covey, Stephen R., The Seven Habits of Highly Effective People, New York: Free Press, Division of Simon & Schuster Inc.,1989.

your resistance is to take note of how you feel when asked to consider a life worth living to its fullest and richest. Do not allow your feelings to become "stuck" and get in the way of changing your mind about what you are able to achieve. It just shows you how attached you are to worry, complaining, and blaming. One woman complained, "I can hardly pay my bills each month, let alone begin to think about how I want to live my life." She could not solve her money problems by staying stuck in her complaining mode and needed to look beyond her immediate concerns to a brighter future.

Other people say they do not want to describe a new lifestyle because they are afraid of being disappointed if they never achieve everything they desire. One man lamented, "I've done this before." When asked to quantify his results, he said that he only got 50 percent of what he had set out to accomplish. Getting half of what he wanted was a great accomplishment, yet he was so focused on what he *did not* accomplish that he was left immobilized.

Still, others have difficulty knowing what they want, yet they are experts at talking about what they do *not* want. Change the things you do not want into a positive and you give your mind a prosperous direction to follow. For example, change the thought, "I do not want financial stress" to a visualization of being financially safe and relaxed. If you are still determined to worry, complain, and blame, and are convinced that life is awful, then you are guaranteed to reap a life of problems and financial drama. Entertain the idea, either in words or in a pictorial vision board, of living the life you desire, and you are more than likely to attain it. Your vision is your roadmap to a life of wealth and wisdom.

A vision doesn't necessarily have to be logical, but it does have to big enough to engage your mind towards the possibilities instead of the worry. Let yourself dream big! You may be astonished at what you can achieve.

The following two Action Items will help you write your vision statement. They encourage you to answer questions including:

- What brings you joy?
- What is it that you want to contribute to others?
- When you leave this planet, what will people say about you?

- Do you want to leave this world a better place than it was when you arrived?
- Are you just a visitor whose life is only a series of bland experiences, or is there a zest for life within you?
- Identify and intensify that zest that lives within you with your written vision statement. Your vision statement is the foundation of your wealth and wisdom, and it will give you guidance, focus, and clarity on your journey to wealth and wisdom.

If you are in a relationship where you share or co-mingle money, it is best if both partners complete their vision statements separately and then compare them. Find the similarities in each person's answers. Use what you have in common to write a third, joint vision statement. Your joint vision helps you to determine spending and savings priorities. Your differences are discussion topics for you to negotiate and come to mutual agreement. One person may envision owning a mountain cabin, for instance, and the other doesn't like the mountains and would prefer a vacation home in Hawaii. Maybe you decide that a few days in the mountains would be great alone time for one partner. You may want to take a couples vacation in Hawaii twice a year rather than own a second home elsewhere. You could also decide that two vacation homes would be just the thing. It doesn't cost any more to write down one vacation home than it does to write down two homes!

Action Item—Vision Statement

As you begin thinking about what you desire, include feeling words that describe what that accomplishment means to your soul. Consider the following example:

My mountain house is a relaxing, quiet, and cozy retreat.
The country girl in me is being cared for and nurtured.

Notice the sense of the mountain cabin and how it feels in addition to the fact of owning a mountain cabin. This vision statement illustrates how the cabin provides the owner with a place of relaxation, quiet, and a sense of nurturance. As you write your vision statement, focus on words that express the experience you truly desire; in doing so, you will paint a word picture of the experience, as well as the material representation. Examples of feeling words include:

Gratitude	Harmony	Peace	Authenticity
Joy	Wholeness	Freedom	Wisdom
Ease	Beauty	Order	Love
Balance	Vitality	Growth	

Action Item—Vision Statement Questions

Here are some vision questions for you to consider as you journey into the imagination of your wealth and wisdom. You need not answer all the questions as they are written; you may combine all your answers into a single paragraph or gather pictures that represent your vision or even combine both methods. If you are more visual, the pictures will give your mind a subconscious message that leads you in the direction of the visual representation. If you decide to do a vision board, make sure you put it where you see it every day. If you are more oriented toward auditory stimulation or a reader by nature, a written vision statement seems to make sense. Also consider that having both modalities available gives your mind a broad wealth path to follow. The categories that follow are intended to help you answer the ultimate questions: "What kind of lifestyle would make you glad to get up in the morning?" and "What suits your soul?" The answers to these two questions are different for everyone. Once you have these answers clear in your wealthy mindset, money is now nothing more than the engine that drives your vision.

Be sure to write your vision statement in the present tense even though it is not your truth for today. A vision statement places a powerful message in your subconscious mind that starts counteracting worry, complaining, and blaming. How to attain your vision will come later in your action steps. Remember, a vision is global in nature and need not be restricted by logic or "what if" thinking. Don't worry, be happy, and have fun with this Action Item.

1. Workday: What is your typical day like now that you have the perfect career/work? What are you doing for most of the day? Who are you talking to and about what are you talking?

2. Self-Care: What are you doing to nurture your physical, spiritual, and mental well-being?

3. Community Service: How are you contributing to the good of the community? What higher purpose or causes sustain you?

4. Home: Where are you living and why? Do you have more than one home? Do you rent or own?

5. Travel: Where and how often do you travel for pleasure and/or business?

6. Health: What do you do to stay active, healthy, and energized? When and how often?

7. Relationship: On what do you base your business/personal relationships? How much of your time do you spend interacting with friends, family, and business associates? Do you need private time to just get away from everybody? If so, how do you accomplish this?

____

____

____

____

____

8. Financial: What do you do with extra money? What financial priorities do you have?

____

____

____

____

____

9. If writing about your ideal life in all of these categories is too big a step for you to do all once, think in terms of five years from now. Use the following example to imagine how you would like your life to be five years from today.

~~~~~~~~~~~~~

Wallet Wisdom Lesson

Balance today's reality
with tomorrow's vision.

~~~~~~~~~~~~~

The Best Year Yet!

Imagine that you are the guest of honor at a Personal Success banquet. You are called to the front of a large room filled with your peers, friends, and family to receive the Award for Extraordinary Personal Success. You will receive the award five years from today. What are you celebrating? Fill in the blanks of this exercise as if the masters of ceremony were introducing you to receive your award.

> *Tonight, we are honoring ________ (your name) for _____ (his or her) ______________ (type of achievement: career, community service, financial, etc.) achievement. In a short period of time, just _________ (time to accomplish), _______ (your name) decided to _____________________________ and has surpassed _____ (his or her) dream(s) beyond _____ (his or her) wildest imagining.*

As you give your acceptance speech, gratefully accepting the award, you might say something similar to the following:

> *It's an honor to be here tonight. I have set my intention to _______________________________. What I discovered once I committed to my intention was nothing short of amazing. Not only has my financial situation improved due to my revenues doubling, but I love my work and have the best employees a person could want. I am fair and generous with them, rewarding their outstanding performance. It gives me great pleasure to see them happy and productive.*
>
> *They return the favor with their loyalty and passion for our work. I have more than enough time for my family, and we take two family vacations together. In fact, we've just returned from _____________. I have a new peace... et cetera.*

Listed below are three questions that may be useful in helping you to unleash the power of your imagination. You may want to answer them as you prepare your "acceptance speech." Remember that these questions have no right answer, as they are designed to help you taste your successful future and make it more real by savoring successes that are to come, so be creative and have fun.

1. What has changed for the better for you in the last five years?

____

____

____

____

____

2. What has significantly improved in your life?

____

____

____

____

____

3. What outstanding issues have been resolved?

____

____

____

____

____

Upon completing all or even part of your vision statement, you might want to read it often. Reading it provides your subconscious with an alternative to worry on which to focus. Your vision becomes your internal motivation, the rainbow beyond the clouds that keeps you going. When talking with others, take a risk and talk about your expected successes instead of your problems and the losses you have suffered. Focus your attention on what you are passionate about, and your behavior will automatically change to support your vision. You simply will not have time to bemoan the fact that life has not always been wonderful. You learn to treat problems as small lessons along the road to wealth and wisdom.

~~~~~~~~~~~~~

Wallet Wisdom Lesson

Spend more time
talking about your dreams
than your drama.

~~~~~~~~~~~~~

By focusing on your vision instead of worrying, complaining, or blaming, you are getting outside of the immediate problem and beginning to think in terms of the possibilities that lie before you. When everyday events attempt to drag you back into the muck of worry or patterns of complaining and blaming, take a moment and revisit your vision statement. Stop and ask yourself what action steps will bring you closer to what you desire. Giving your thought process a new focus lightens up the worry and makes complaining and blaming a thing of the past.

You will notice this change in your thinking and behavior very quickly once you refuse to be a helpless victim of circumstances. The second lesson on your way to wealth and wisdom asks you explore and understand how assumptions, judgments, and negative attitudes prevent you from generating and receiving the money necessary to achieve the life you desire.

Chapter

2 There's More Than One Way...

I agree to be creative, open and flexible to generating and receiving money.

As you were growing up, you observed and, to a large degree, absorbed the money habits and beliefs your family practiced. What you were taught about money by word or example, past personal experiences, and generally accepted cultural attitudes (often called the collective consciousness), as well as peer pressure, all have helped to form your ideas about how you get money and what you can and cannot do with it.

These ideas and attitudes about money determine your *money beliefs*. Your money beliefs govern how much money you will have and how you will use the money available to you. Etched into your thinking process, these beliefs are like concrete, forming rigid thinking. Rigid thinking driven by an unconscious a set of beliefs will stop you in your prosperity journey. It is the number one thing that gets in the way of achieving wealth without ever being aware of the influence these beliefs have over your wealth potential.

Most people have never examined their money beliefs to determine if they are relevant or even accurate. Unconsciously accepted money beliefs are their only reality. They live by these rigid attitudes that determine their behaviors regarding money, its uses, and abuses. Perhaps what they believe is just the result of stories passed down from generation to generation with no basis in fact. Maybe, just maybe, time is *not* money and money is actually easy to get, despite the fact that all the axioms tell us otherwise. Is it possible to be rich without being selfish, greedy, or shallow? If you have negative, predetermined ideas about rich people, then you will find subconscious ways to keep a significant amount of money from coming your way. If you have decided that having a significant amount of money automatically makes you corrupt or that vast sums of money can only be had by ripping off those who are less fortunate, you have created an internal mental glass ceiling. Be assured that you will never attain anything beyond the amount you've given yourself mental permission to have. If for some reason you have an extraordinary financial success, you will probably find a way to lose the money in some convoluted manner as a way to protect yourself from your negative beliefs about rich people.

~~~~~~~~~~~~~

Wallet Wisdom Lesson

People do
weird things with money,
they just DO!

~~~~~~~~~~~~~

Understanding your assumptions about money at a deeper level involves delving into their roots of origin. Questioning the accuracy of these assumptions is like shedding an old scarcity shell that has been built around your inner being.

Based on such assumptions, you may have decided early on that there is only one way to generate money. The job holder becomes dependent on the almighty paycheck, and the business owner on the assumption that profitability is hard won. However, if you open yourself to the possibility of money appearing in ways you never imagined, magical things might happen. Imagine money coming to you in unexpected and untraditional ways, maybe through an unexpected gift, getting a larger raise than anticipated, or closing a major account. There also is the old adage that it is better to give than to receive; Giving from your extra abundant wealth is distinct and different than giving as a martyr to an old belief. Mary was a willing victim to her belief that loyalty to her boss was a means of generating more money—until she closely examined that belief. She was suffering in a job that was far below her financial comfort zone. She continued to live with the daily stress and anxiety caused by her job because she had strong, fixed ideas about how money is generated. Mary truly wanted a stable, consistent income, but she felt such an accomplishment was impossible to achieve in her current job situation. She was working on straight commission, selling large ticket industrial items and getting paid on a monthly basis. Her income would vary depending on her sales that month. Sometimes she received what she considered a large check, while other months she received very little money.

She insisted that she was doomed to be in constant stress about money. Would she have enough to last the month? Would she blow it when she got a large check? Over and over again she remarked that there was simply no way out of her dilemma. Unfortunately, Mary's rigidity and sense of looming tragedy kept her from considering another job, working on increasing her sales, or learning to better manage her commission checks.

The loyalty part of Mary's belief required her to remain committed to *one* employer no matter the circumstances. This loyalty remained firm in her thinking, so much so that she was unable to take any positive action steps. What would have happened to Mary's life if she had multiple income streams? Where and when did she learn the rule that says you must be loyal to only one boss for your income?

Determined to change her money belief system, Mary finally decided to get creative by starting her own business in addition to her current position. She liked the idea of being her own boss during the weekends. In the process of starting her side business, she signed up for a management program at the local community college. In the course of that program, she met a guidance counselor who volunteered to help her update her resume. As she was opening up to new ideas about how to generate money, her sales began to pick up as well. Customers liked her positive attitude and they started giving her referrals. Mary wondered why this had never happened before, until she realized that she was actually more interested in her customers' well-being now that she was using her entrepreneurial creativity to generate additional money. She certainly didn't feel scared or depressed as she had when she continually feared running out of money. Mary's multiple income stream provided the opportunity for increased income, erased her old thinking pattern that there is only way to generate money, and gave her a sense of freedom she had never before experienced.

Many of the traditional, worn out, and outdated beliefs about money that people carry dissolve when they are subjected to the light of day. The cherished belief that time is money was ingrained into American culture at the beginning of the Industrial Revolution in the late 1800's. Before that time, farmers followed the rhythms of season, not the clock, and families provided for each other in old age. However, the Industrial Revolution necessitated a different way of life. In the face of rapidly advancing mechanization, employers and employees entered into an unspoken agreement. Employees traded their productive time for money as well as their loyalty to one employer—for the promise of a safe, secure retirement with pension.

~~~~~~~~~~~~~

Wallet Wisdom Lesson

Conventional money wisdom
is not always wise.

~~~~~~~~~~~~~

Times certainly have changed, but even with all the evidence of layoffs and downsizing, the beliefs about work and money remain the same for Alice and thousands of others like her. Alice is a dynamic young woman who was caught in an underpaid job. Her boss even refused to pay for her reasonable and allowable business expenses. Furthermore, he had reduced her monthly base salary during a time when she was ill and not as productive as he felt she needed to be. For a long time, she felt she was unable to get out of this financially abusive situation.

Beginning to realize the emotional and economic toll that this job was taking, Alice thought about why she felt impelled to stay in a less than satisfactory position. Once she began to evaluate her situation, she realized that because her father had only one job in his entire career, she had inherited his narrow idea of the job market. Alice believed she should work for only one company for her entire career and that leaving her job meant she was uncommitted and lacked the necessary tenacity to endure trials at work. It was not until she understood that this moldy old belief was outdated that Alice was able to update her resume and begin a new job search.

A variety of hidden beliefs (and sometimes those that are not so hidden) about the rights and wrongs of earning money will get in the way of creating a Wealthy U. John heard more than once as he was growing up that "money doesn't grow on trees," as well as "neither a borrower nor a lender be." As a result of these messages, John learned that there were simply no gray areas where money was concerned. Still, John had always dreamed of opening up his own business and found that he needed the capital to do so. Knowing this, a few of John's friends who shared his vision for his business offered to loan him the necessary funds.

Immediately, he responded to the offer by telling his friends that he could not possibly borrow money from them, drawing upon his long-held belief that it was simply *not right to borrow money from friends*. If he had borrowed the money to go on a spending spree, he might have had a point. However, his limited view of what is right and wrong kept him from receiving money that could have generated more money and allowed him to repay his friends with interest. He refused the loan, even though his friends believed in him and truly wanted to help him. His lack of creative, flexible thinking kept him financially "stuck."

Even when you become more aware of the negative and limiting attitudes and beliefs that determine your behaviors, shifting your money belief system is a process that takes time and commitment. Imagine for moment that someone puts your trash basket in a different spot. Chances are, you will continue going to the original place where your trash container once sat. The trash might even end up on the floor until someone moves the container back to the original location. Eventually you will realize that the trash container has been moved and the papers will fall into it with ease and no forethought. Making changes in your money thinking is a huge undertaking when compared to moving a trash container. But unlike moving the trash container, emptying the trash from your head does make significant changes in your finances.

Those old worn out beliefs are like concrete that you are chipping away with your self-awareness. Gradually, over time, the concrete of old beliefs is worn down and finally disappears as you move along the road to attaining both the wealth you deserve and the wisdom to use it well. Even making what might be considered small changes puts the process into motion and leads to bigger more positive changes in your complex, and mostly negative, money-belief system.

~~~~~~~~~~~~~

Wallet Wisdom Lesson

Small, consistent action steps
lead to a track record of successes.
A track record of successes leads
to self trust, and self trust leads to
wealth & wisdom.

~~~~~~~~~~~~~

You might start with something small, such as a dinner tab, for example. How many times has someone offered to pick up a dinner tab and you've refused? You may have done this because your pride would not let you accept a gift, or you have been taught that if someone gives you something, they probably expect something in return. But have you considered that this person may value you as friend, associate, or customer, and paying the tab is simply a way to show that appreciation? Perhaps you have never learned to graciously receive gifts of money. When faced with this situation or others like it, practice saying, "Yes, thank you." If others are always taking you to dinner, it is equally powerful to change that behavior by picking up the tab yourself once in a while. Creating a balance between giving and receiving is a lesson well learned in opening up your receptivity quotient and allowing yourself to receive greater amounts of money in wonderful and unusual ways.

You might even try the same strategy that Bob used. Each time someone invited him to be a guest at lunch or dinner, he put $20 in an envelope. At the end of the month, he was surprised to have over $200 in his envelope. This money would not have been available to him had he not learned how to accept a gift. He was willing to entertain the idea that he could be masculine and still open his mind to new ways of thinking, even though his father had taught him that it wasn't manly to let someone else pay for dinner.

Like Bob, you probably learned much of what you know about money, and what you do *not* know about money, from the people who raised you. Well-meaning though they were, the people who raised you passed on what they had learned from their parents either by word or their actions. Your grandparents passed on what they had learned through hard won experience, and so it goes even today. Few people have received a rational, systematic money education. Even if you had a personal money management class in school, chances are you were far more influenced by the money behaviors of your parents than anything you learned in a class.

The exact origin of generational money beliefs is difficult to determine except that they are based on past history and experiences. For example, the Great Depression of the 1930's had a profound impact on the people who lived through it. More than any other event of the twentieth century, the Depression was a time of serious deprivation and financial trauma. Financial safety nets that we rely on today—such as welfare, social security, and Medicare—did not exist. Some people chose to end their lives rather than face financial ruin. The impact of the 1930's Depression is still felt to this day in many of our money beliefs, maybe not quite as dramatic or personal as Sarah's, but with just as much power to affect wealth potential.

Sarah's mother always cautioned her about keeping an ample supply of food in the house. Her mother was a child during the Depression and had horrible memories of going to bed hungry. These memories left an indelible imprint that Sarah's mother unknowingly passed on to her daughter. In the mother's thinking, it was just a matter of time until another disaster threatened her survival and that of her children. Determined to protect Sarah, her mother told her over and over and again to be prepared because, "You never know when we could have another Depression or disaster." Sarah heard the same message hundreds of times during her formative years. Her mother did not intend any harm in passing on her concerns, but an unintended consequence was that Sarah not only made a point to stock the freezer, but she was always afraid she would not have enough money. This caused her to fear leaving her low-paying job for a better one with no seniority, and stopped her from exploring a non-traditional investment that would generate considerably more money than a traditional savings account. Sarah had no control over her financial destiny as long as she was living her mother's beliefs.

Sarah began to realize the burden of the money legacy she had received from her mother. She decided to take steps to rid herself of these fears by going home and cleaning out the freezer. She felt this would be a good first step; symbolic of throwing away old ideas along with the outdated, frozen goods that bulged from her freezer. While Sarah wasn't subjected to the trauma of living through the Depression, she had preserved the beliefs that arose as a result of that troubled time. She reported having a physical reaction as she reached into the freezer with trembling hands. That small voice was saying, "What will your mother think? You are going to starve." Rather than argue with the voice, she continued to clear out the freezer despite the shaking hands. Once she identified her unconscious belief, she was able to understand the power of its influence on her thinking and take a symbolic action step to release herself from the negativity and fear that held her back.

Like Sarah, Ryan allowed his money beliefs to limit his options. Ryan had been a top-level executive, but due to corporate downsizing, he was now working for minimum wage. As a result of this significant reduction in his income, he lost his house and his dignity in the process. He considered himself "homeless," as he was staying with friends who had made it clear from the start that it would be a short-term stay. When he was asked to move out, he simply did not know what he was going to do and was seriously thinking about living in his car.

Ryan explained that he had few assets, noting, however, that he did have $12,000 in his company savings (retirement) account. Common sense would seem to dictate that he access the $12,000 because he was in the middle of a financial thunderstorm, a real "rainy day." Still, he was being controlled by the old piggy bank message that told him it was foolish to withdraw the money because he would be subject to an early withdrawal penalty. While accessing retirement funds is not usually the best advice, his circumstances were anything but usual at the moment. All his life he had been conditioned to save for a rainy day, but nowhere in his conditioning had he learned to define a rainy day and give himself permission to use the money he had saved as he found himself in dire circumstances.

As in the cases of Sarah and Ryan, parents sometimes say and do destructive things that they have no idea limit your ability to generate and receive money. In fact, many people were raised in what might be characterized as a financially dysfunctional home. Perhaps you are one of those people. Maybe your parents continually argued about money, or perhaps you can recall few, if any, calm, rational discussions about the subject. Instead, when you think about money discussions at all, you remember loud accusations about spending and the fact that there was not enough money for this or that. Money was typically a subject of great distress and anxiety. As a result, you reached the natural conclusion, without actually being consciously aware of it, that money causes problems.

If you believe that money causes problems, why would you want to acquire more of it? People who build themselves up to a certain level of income and then lose it all only to repeat the process over and over again may have had this as one of their negative money beliefs. They will sabotage themselves to fulfill their belief that *money causes problems*. These people have created their own problems by believing that money is the cause of problems and that more money simply means greater headaches. They have emotional permission to earn a certain amount and no more. Whatever your thoughts about money, they warrant a deeper look at your own hidden beliefs.

For every negative thing you learned about money, there are literally hundreds of others hidden in your subconscious mind. Exposing hidden, rigid, and negative money beliefs opens up your creativity, generating ideas for greater opportunities. Wonderful magical surprises, and unexpected gifts of money tend to show up naturally. Identifying and dealing with the hidden messages makes you more creative, open, and flexible, which in turn makes it easier to attract money in ways you have never imagined.

Literally millions of money myths exist because the entire monetary system is based on the belief in scarcity. Scarcity of money is what supposedly makes it valuable, but it is that belief and the extension of that belief that generates the collective negative beliefs. Acceptance of the collective scarcity belief collapses your openness, flexibility, and creativity for generating and receiving money.

A few of the more common collective money myths are listed below:

Myth: *I can't make money by doing what I love.*

The hidden message: Making money is separate from real life.

The reality: Studies show that millionaires love what they do and often say that work is their hobby.

The truth: True wealth comes from being passionately involved in contributing something to the world.

Myth: *Men make money and women spend it.*

The hidden message: Women are irresponsible with money.

The reality: Men can overspend just as easily as women.

The truth: Irresponsible spending is not gender-specific.

Myth: *Having more money automatically solves problems.*

The hidden message: Money in and of itself has power.

The reality: Throwing money at problems doesn't solve them. It just masks them and sometimes adds more zeros to the debt.

The truth: True wealth comes from being self-confident, self-directed, and having faith in our own abilities.

Myth: *Money buys love, happiness, et cetera.*

The hidden message: You can buy love and happiness at the store.

The reality: Just pick up the newspaper on any given day. Many very rich and famous people find themselves in serious personal and financial straits. In fact, even many lottery winners are deeply in debt.

The truth: Money gives us more choices and nothing else.

Myth: *Money is the root of all evil.*

The hidden message: Having money is evil.

The reality: The accurate quote is: "The love of (or lust for) money is the root of all evil."

The truth: Money is neither good nor evil. Money has no character traits at all.

You have the freedom to make new and better choices that will cause money to become a prosperous, nurturing, peaceful, and harmonious part of your life.

Which of these myths have affected your wealth potential? Are there any other money myths you would like to eliminate from your belief system? Perhaps you have longstanding myths about rich people. Some people believe that when you are rich, everyone wants your money, that you have to buy your friends, or that you will automatically have problems with drugs and alcohol. Another "rich people" myth is that if you are wealthy, you live in constant fear of losing your money, friends, or spouse, or that everyone will be jealous of you. You also may believe that in order to be rich, you would not have time for things you enjoy, including spending time with family.

Even if you don't think you believe any of the above, it makes sense to embrace the possibility of being truly wealthy by digging into your subconscious mind and telling yourself the truth. Do you believe all rich people are corrupt, pushy, miserable, spoiled, greedy, or cheap? If so, then how creative and open are you to being truly wealthy? The reality is that none of the words typically attributed to rich people are necessarily any truer of rich people than of poor people. It is not money that determines a person's behavior; it is the *person* and their determination of how money will be used. In fact, having more than enough money gives people the opportunity to give back to the world in some tremendous ways.

Action Items

In order to better understand your current money flexibility as it affects your behaviors and attitudes, complete the following Action Items. The answers will give you insight as to how your past history influences your flexibility, creativity, and openness to even the possibility of wealth. Your answers are for your own self-awareness so you can make new and better choices about money and wealth. As always, there are no right or wrong answers. There is nothing to be embarrassed about if you are not able to answer all of the questions. The information probably was not available to you, because many families do not talk about money in front of children. If you were raised in two or more households due to divorce, death, or other circumstances, pick the one situation that you spent the most time in or that had the greatest influence on you, and work from there. As you might imagine, because money ranks in the top three stated reasons for divorce, being raised in two households could likely cause mixed money messages to be part of your financial upbringing. One parent may have been financially conservative while the other spent freely, often out of guilt or to win affection. You might find that mixed messages and other patterns are disclosed after answering the questions below.

Simply answer those that apply to you to the best of your ability.

Father's Attitude

1. How did your father spend money?

____

____

____

____

____

2. What did he say, teach, or imply about money?

3. What were his spending priorities?

4. Even if your father was not present during your childhood, what conclusions did you draw regarding men and money?

Mother's Attitude

1. How did your mother spend money?

2. What did she say, teach, or imply about money?

3. What were her spending priorities?

4. Even if your mother was not present during your childhood, what conclusions did you draw regarding money and women?

Family Attitudes: Gifts

Try to recall a gift that you were promised when you were a child, but you did not receive, or received a substitution instead. It could be a birthday present or some other agreed upon or promised gift.

1. What was the gift?

2. Did you ask for it?

3. If so, what (if anything) was said or not said about the broken promise?

____

____

____

____

____

4. If you did not ask about the broken promise, explain why.

____

____

____

____

____

5. Were any conditions attached to getting or not getting the gift? For example, did you have to earn part of the money or be a good kid for a certain amount of time or get a good grade?

____

____

____

____

____

6. Assuming you met the terms laid out to receive the gift, were the agreements kept or broken?

7. What conclusions did you reach regarding receiving gifts?

Family Attitudes: Crises

1. Recall a financial crisis that occurred in your family. What happened?

2. How old were you?

3. How did your mother react?

4. How did your father react?

5. What decision(s) did you make about money after that event?

____

____

____

____

____

6. What else can you remember about how your family interacted with money?

____

____

____

____

____

Debriefing Family Attitudes

1. What general conclusions did you draw from the previous exercise about your family's beliefs, ideas, and myths regarding money?

____

____

____

____

____

2. What hidden messages did you receive about gifts, money, and their uses?

3. What were the underlying uses of money in your home? Was it used to control or to manipulate? Was it used for survival or for security? Was it used to express anger, love, or some other emotion?

4. How have you been affected by these money behaviors?

5. What did your parents teach you about money that you would like to incorporate into your life?

____

____

____

____

____

Perhaps you have never considered how personal past history developed your thoughts and habits about money. As you worked your way through these insightful questions, you may have had some "ah ha" moments. The insights you received are a true blessing as they allow you to understand, at a deeper level, not only your hidden beliefs about money, but also the origin of those beliefs. You might even marvel at how well you have managed your financial life given the negative, stale money baggage you've been carrying around. The awareness you have gained of those past experiences and ideas and how they shaped your current money reality has cleaned the slate for making new and wealthier choices about money. You are not doomed by your past any more than these past negative beliefs have any power to determine your future. Self-awareness in and of itself helps dump outworn, negative, and dated head trash—giving you inner permission to have significant dollars in a positive lighthearted manner.

Now that you are more self-aware of how old moldy ideas have affected your wealth potential, the next step in changing your thinking about money is to turn the negative into a positive statement that counteracts the old beliefs. The following Action Item will help you do just that by turning a negative into a positive affirming statement.

Action Item—Turnaround Statement

Directions: Think of the one negative limiting money belief that most surprised you or made you the most uncomfortable while doing the exercises above. Answer the following questions to the best of your ability. Do not be concerned with all the other past beliefs that limit you. Just focus on the one that you think had the most impact on you today, leaving the others for another time. Read the examples below before starting your own to get an idea of how it is done.

Example 1:

My negative or limiting belief about money is—I'll never have enough money.

The way in which it limits me is—I never seem to have enough money.

The way I want to be, act, or feel is—I want to be safe and secure with enough money to pay my bills and have some extra for fun stuff.

My turnaround statement is—I am safe and secure with enough money to pay for my needs, wants, and desires.

Example 2:

My negative or limiting belief about money is—Money just seems to slip through my fingers. I am a lousy money manager or I just can't control my money.

The way in which it limits me is—I never seem to know where my money goes each month.

The way I want to be, act or feel is—I want to be in control of my money and know that I can mange it well.

My turnaround statement is—I am in control of my money and have excellent money management skills.

Use the following guideline questions to write your own turnaround statement

1. My negative or limiting idea about money is:

2. The way in which it limits me is:

3. The way I want to be, act, or feel is:

4. My turnaround statement is: (As in the examples above, a turnaround statement begins with the words "I am." The statement is written in the present tense even if it is not true today, because it is the direction you intend on taking, so you are making a positive, affirming statement about it).

____

____

____

____

____

Use the positive affirming statement above to check in with your creativity, flexibility, and openness to generating and receiving money. By now you know that mixed messages about money abound, and these types of messages contribute to a narrow and inflexible view of money. You have begun the process of changing your thinking about money by closely examining the hidden beliefs underlying your attitude toward money. As you shed your old, rigid ideas, be ready for life to move forward in ways you never imagined.

As you open up your creativity and flexibility, you may find that there are unresolved money matters from the past or present that you have been neglecting. Openness and flexibility can generate new ways of looking at money, but paying attention to details and staying current with your finances builds trust in your ability to handle having lots more money.

Chapter

3 Get Your Financial House in Order

I agree to be current and complete on all financial transactions.

Carrying around unresolved money issues is like dragging a ball and chain with you everywhere you go. Old money habits and worn out ideas and beliefs die a much faster death when you replace them with positive, workable money behaviors. Becoming aware of the tangled money web woven by personal conditioning is a significant step, but all the analysis, understanding, and awareness mean nothing without positive change. For example, if you insist on justifying inappropriate money behaviors because your parents didn't provide a strong example of money management, or if you are still rebelling against your past, then you remain a victim to your past. The most effective way to stop repeating the past is to take active steps towards living in the present by being up to date and current with your financial transactions.

Excuses for not being current and complete are many and varied. Do you ever find yourself saying or thinking self-defeating thoughts such as, "I'm just too busy" to pay attention to money? Do you wonder what difference it makes if you know the details of your finances? Do you live in hope that things will just work out by themselves? Have you uttered any of these statements, or something like them? "I don't have very much money, so what difference does it make?" "I don't like what I see when I look at my finances, so it's easier not to look at them." "So what if I don't balance my bank statement this month, I can always do it next month or the month after that." "I have better things to do than spend time messing with money paperwork." By continually allowing yourself to indulge in this type of evasive self-talk, you are unconsciously sending yourself a powerful, negative, mental message. You are literally telling yourself that you cannot be trusted to respect and steward vast sums of money. At the same time, you are reinforcing old self-defeating beliefs and practicing the same old financial behaviors.

The combination of negative self-talk, excuses, and avoidance is deadly to generating wealth and wisdom. Being current and complete with the amount of money you presently possess prepares you mentally and emotionally to have larger amounts of money. What if you had millions to take care of each day? Would you trust the bank or anyone else to never make a mistake with your vast holdings? Would you behave differently if you had a large investment portfolio? If you answered yes to the last question, then start now to behave as if you already had vast sums of money. Set the stage to having wealth by choosing to be current and complete as part of your everyday experience.

Some people think they only can be current and complete when they know everything there is to know about money or can predict the future and avoid unplanned circumstances. These people are really not current and complete because past fears still drive their need to know all the answers. Being current and complete simply means that you are familiar and up to date with *all* of your financial matters. It does not necessarily mean you have zero balances on all credit cards, but it does mean you know the total balance, open the bills each month, know when they are due, and pay them on time or make arrangements with any creditor if you are going to be late. Being current is taking responsibility for growing your wealth potential. The word "responsibility" can carry a lot of weight—as it is a word that can evoke feelings of guilt and shame for past mistakes. But in its truest sense, it simply means "the ability to respond."

The Illusion

Avoidance is a form of financial dysfunction, whether it takes the form of failing to open your bills or pretending you have lots of money by picking up the tab for all your friends, even if you are on the financial edge. Borrowing money with no intention of paying it back also is a form of dysfunction. Prosperous change means being honest with yourself by becoming aware of the way denial and avoidance of your true financial situation impacts you and those around you. The very nature of denial is that the person does not usually realize they are in denial. Unfortunately, many people do not realize they are in denial until a crisis hits. If you are living in denial, any little change in your life can send you over the edge. The restaurant turning down a maxed out credit card in front your friends is embarrassing in and of itself, but what if the electric company shuts off your electricity because you failed to pay the bill? Failing to be current and complete by not paying attention to day-to-day money matters makes money crises even more dramatic and slams your mental doors to having more money.

Carrying around unresolved money issues is like carrying around an invisible sack of emotional garbage that affects your wealth potential in ways you cannot begin to imagine. You may look and act no different than those around you, but you are actually still living with past fears, past mistakes, past beliefs. The unconscious fear is that you may find out something about yourself and your money that you would rather not know. One couple who was ready to face this fear was delighted to find that they could gain control of their money simply by tracking their weekly expenses. They agreed to write down (on a pre-prepared list) what they spent each day. This grid was separated by category, giving them a visual picture of their weekly spending habits. At the end of the second week of this assignment, their tracking sheet was as blank as day one. When asked about it, they came up with one of many typical excuses that people use to avoid their fears. “We got too busy,” they said, thinking that answer would suffice. But when questioned further, they admitted, somewhat sheepishly, that they were afraid to know what was going on financially because of what they might find out about themselves. They never considered that they might have found that they were being reasonable and rational in their spending habits. They had just assumed they were incapable of controlling their money.

Avoidance of being current and complete helped to reinforce their old money story; the story that told them they were destined to mess up. They got a pleasant surprise once they began writing down what they were spending. They made a few minor changes, stopped wasting so much time arguing about who was spending what, and got on with their lives. They were able to begin to understand the idea of planning for a more prosperous future. What's more, by being current and complete, they gained dignity and financial self-respect. In turn, this self-respect and confidence taught the couple that they are capable of managing even larger amounts of money.

If you have the courage to "get real" as this couple did, you are further preparing your mental groundwork for wealth and wisdom. Getting real may involve trudging through the dark depths of a past that can clutter your emotional, physical, and mental space. When was the last time you gave your dusty, dark, hidden, financial closet a spring cleaning? Stuffing new clothes into a closet full of old, worn-out items shares similarities with your "money closet," though you may have to dig deeper in your mental closet to find those things that are hidden and forgotten.

This type of "spring cleaning" is illustrated by the oft-repeated story of a young man who wanted to know the secret of life. He traveled far and wide and ended up in a distant land where there lived a man called the "Guru of Universal Truth." Once there, he requested a meeting, and after waiting several days, he was finally admitted to see the revered guru. Before the young man uttered even one question, the guru invited him to tea. The guru poured the tea into the young man's cup and kept pouring until the teacup was filled and overflowing. As the tea splashed onto the floor, the young man yelled, "Stop, my cup is full." The guru replied, "I cannot give you the answer to your question, as into a full cup I can pour nothing new." The lesson being taught to the young man was that in order to have room for new ideas you must clear out the old ones; you need to have space for new ideas to take root. Making space—both physical and mental—for wealth and wisdom works the same way.

Cleaning your financial closet and keeping it clean clears your mental and physical space for wealth. Remember the last time you cleaned your closet or garage? Suddenly there was empty space for new things where none existed before. Similarly, a gardener understands the need to cut back and get rid of the dead flowers so new ones can grow even more abundantly. If you do not prune back the dead foliage, there is no room for new blossoms. Staying up to date and current with your financial matters works in much the same way. It is impossible to have a financially healthy and truly wealthy life while hanging onto to moldy old habits and "stuff."

People who cling to old, unused things usually have a difficult time letting go of their emotional past as well, including their negative emotions of resentment, hurt, blame, and sadness. People who hold on to money-centered dramas, fears, and denial are cluttering the space meant for wealth just as if they were filling a closet with more junk. Being current and complete is the lesson that makes mental space for new opportunities to come into your life, because your prosperity cup is no longer overflowing with clutter.

Symbolically, "making space for new opportunities" may be as simple as cleaning out your old files so you can find what you need when you need it. Get rid of receipts and other papers that you no longer need. If you are unsure if you will need something in the future, start an archiving system; put the things out of sight that you are unlikely to need on a consistent basis.

You are being current and complete by simply making arrangements to pay all outstanding debts, including back taxes. As difficult as it can sometimes be, being current and complete also means repaying loans received from family or friends. While it is typically best to pay interest-bearing obligations first, sometimes money borrowed from family or friends comes with very high emotional interest, as was the case for one newly married couple who owed $1500 to the young man's parents. Before they married, Clay's parents had helped him pay for several summer college courses and the books needed for the classes. As kind as it was for Clay's parents to loan him the money, neither he nor his parents had made any arrangements for repaying it. Instead, his parents presumed that Clay would repay the money when he was able.

When he graduated from college and got settled into his career, Clay and his wife began to purchase items for their home and to spend money on recreation—from eating out to going on vacations. Still, no matter how much time passed, a nagging feeling remained. In fact, every time Clay's parents came to their house, he and his wife felt guilty about having purchased something new. They avoided talking about any subject that might reveal how they had spent extra money. While the loan was sizeable enough that it would have been difficult for them to pay it in one lump sum, it was reasonable for them to propose a workable repayment plan. To further complicate matters, Clay's parents never directly asked for the money, but they continually joked about the debt.

This situation was burdensome not only to Clay and his wife, but also to Clay's parents. The couple kept themselves in emotional bondage by failing to acknowledge the debt, and the parents, who rightfully wished to be repaid, felt they couldn't broach the subject. You, too, may have been afraid or hesitant to bring up a subject you wish would just disappear, but fear and hesitancy do nothing to help you build your bank account any faster. Instead of avoidance, take a risk and address the issue in a manner that is honest and sincere. Even if you are unable to pay your obligations immediately, you become current and complete when each party understands the obligation and the arrangements for repayment.

Inform the person to whom you owe money of your present financial situation and let them know when they can expect payment. Propose a payment plan that is less than the amount you think you can pay, so you can ensure that you will make good on your promise. You can always repay a debt earlier than expected. In addition to laying out a specific repayment plan, express your appreciation for the money that was loaned, even if you don't feel appreciative at the moment. As difficult as it might be to repay the loan, keep in mind that you are paying it as much for your own financial integrity as for the other person's pocketbook.

By making these arrangements and following through with them, you will be relieved of the guilt that has accompanied the unpaid loan. What's more, you will begin to have more confidence in your other financial transactions because you are no longer being dishonest with yourself. For Clay and his wife, paying off their debt eliminated an unspoken anxiety and allowed them to find more joy in having a meal out together or finding a treasure for their home.

Another form of avoidance that prevents you from being current and complete is to deny your own financial needs to fulfill the financial needs of others. Tom's adult children moved in with him for what was supposed to be a temporary stay. Tom's son had lost his job, and because his son and his wife had a new baby, Tom felt obligated to help out where he could. Besides, he was lonely after his wife of 45 years died suddenly. At first glance it seemed like an ideal arrangement for all concerned. However, while having company had its benefits, Tom soon realized that he would have also enjoyed some solitude. He began to date a woman he had known for years whose husband had died, but he felt strange inviting her to his home since he didn't have much privacy. He soon began to resent paying all the bills and providing the food. Yes, he liked his daughter-in-law's cooking, but something was just not working. He felt guilty and selfish for wanting his quiet home back, yet was conflicted by enjoying the company of his children. Tom and his son had made no agreement as to how much time he would live at his father's home or when he would begin contributing to the expenses.

Tom wanted to be seen as caring and compassionate, but he feared appearing selfish or ungrateful for the company. Finally, he took the risk and asked himself some important questions before he talked with his son. Did Tom expect payment for all the help he had provided? Was Tom making it a gift or a draw against any inheritance? Tom began by talking with his adult children, cleaning up hidden resentments, and being up-front about his need for privacy. His children were relieved to hear Tom wouldn't mind it if they moved within the next year. They had been feeling guilty for wanting a home of their own and shamed by what they saw as taking unfair advantage of dad. Tom was draining his financial and emotional resources in the hope that his kids would love and appreciate him. Instead, he could have been on the receiving end of their passive anger if he had not taken action.

Tom became current and complete by breaking through his avoidance. You may not have children living with you, but it is impossible to be current and complete without stopping financially co-dependent behaviors such as allowing teenagers to use your credit card, co-signing for notes, and so on. Collect or make arrangements for payment of the money owed to you. Pretending a friend you gave a loan to had never borrowed the money does nothing to help him or her, *or* you. As an alternative, propose a manageable payment agreement, put it in writing, and have both of you sign it. If you believe that the money will never be paid, or if you feel you are truly ready to "let go" of the money, get it out of your mental closet by making it a gift and sending a letter absolving the debt. It may be useful to do this when you file next year's taxes. The lesson is to bring the debt out of the closet of secrecy.

Other strategies for becoming current and complete include making sure you write agreements for all current financial transactions, including personal loans, so that your closet doesn't fill up again. Also, if you have not balanced your checkbook in awhile, consider getting one of the many computer software programs that make it easy, or ask a trusted friend to help you. Set aside a time each month to take care of your money management strategies.

Sometimes people carry needless guilt around with them for years, subconsciously holding themselves back from achieving their dreams. Having taken some effective action towards being current and complete, the next step is to go inside and forgive yourself and others for any past financial wrongdoing—what you truly forgive can never hurt you. Ellen revealed that she felt still guilty about a bankruptcy she had filed several years earlier, seemingly making her afraid to make too much money because she feared blowing it again. For Ellen, the best thing she can do is to make a list of the lessons learned from her past and bring herself current and complete internally as well as externally. You will know you've forgiven yourself when 1) you make new and different choices about how you behave with money and 2) you have very little to say about it and spend none of your emotional energy even thinking about the past perceived mistake.

~~~~~~~~~~~~~

Wallet Wisdom Lesson

The best way to heal the past
is to get on with the present and
do it differently.

~~~~~~~~~~~~~

Because most of us are our own worst critics, forgiveness is a concept that sounds good in theory, but is something that is fraught with negative self-judgment. Think of forgiveness as being current and complete with past mistakes. Write yourself a letter expressing how you feel about your past financial experiences, both your successes and your shortcomings. Include what you've learned from each experience. You might do any of the three Action Items that follow in order to forgive yourself more fully.

Action Item

Fear of repeating a past financial mistake often keeps you from having the wealth you desire. One way to break through this fear is to learn from past mistakes, forgive them, and make different choices in the future. The following exercises will help you do just that.

Step 1—Debriefing Failures

Recall a financial dream, vision, or goal that you did not accomplish. Select one that you still talk or think about. Answer the following questions to the best of your ability.

1. What incident or situation in my relationship to money have I not forgiven?

____

____

____

____

____

2. How do I think and feel about this particular situation?

____

____

____

____

____

3. What things outside of me and beyond my control contributed to this situation?

____

____

____

____

____

4. What things within me or within my control helped to create this situation?

____

____

____

____

____

5. What am I learning about my relationship to money?

____

____

____

____

____

6. Which of the seven lessons will assist me to make better choices in the future?

____

____

____

____

____

7. What immediate action steps can I take to put what I've learned in this exercise into action?

____

____

____

____

____

Step 2—Debriefing Successes

Recall a financial dream, vision, or goal that you have accomplished. Choose one about which you feel especially proud. Answer the following questions.

1. What financial goal, dream, or vision did I accomplish?

____

____

____

____

2. How do I feel about this accomplishment?

3. What challenges or obstacles did I face on the path to my accomplishment?

4. What internal resources did I mobilize to break through these obstacles?

5. What external resources did I access to support my accomplishment?

____

____

____

____

____

6. Which of the lessons or other agreements I make with myself will help assure my future success?

____

____

____

____

____

7. What am I learning about myself that will contribute to the success of my future goals and intentions?

____

____

____

____

____

Step 3—Comparing Success to Failure

The only real failure is failing to learn from your mistakes, and in effect, preventing yourself from moving on. When comparing what you call failures to what you call successes, you will see some behaviors that work well in creating wealth, and some that you'd rather discard.

1. What are the similarities or differences between your successes and your failures?

____

____

____

____

2. What patterns, if any, have you discovered about your success and failure?

____

____

____

____

3. Which past behaviors assisted you in your accomplishments? How can you use these same behaviors in the future?

____

____

____

____

____

Letting go of the past means:

- I accept that I can't do anything about it.
- I realize that I can't control my past.
- I learn from the consequences of my mistakes and do not repeat them.
- I allow myself to be human.
- I accept myself completely.
- I trust myself to make reasonable and rational financial decisions.
- I trust myself to become what I dream I can be.
- I trust myself to have wealth and wisdom.

Take a moment to bless your past mistakes for being good teachers and then let them fade into history. Doing so is the internal part—the soul part—of being current and complete. Wealth is generated in the present, not in the past. Current and complete means that you are present and engaged in productive activities that generate money today and in the future.

Take time each day to give thanks for the money you already have, and then show that appreciation by actively honoring and respecting your money. You may never be a person who looks forward to paying bills, but it is a very good habit to be appreciative of the fact that you have the money to pay for goods and services already provided. Appreciating and being a good steward of the money you already have leads to trusting yourself to have vast sums of money. Part of respecting the money you already have means that you pay attention to your buying motives as well as to what and how you spend money.

Chapter

4 Guilt-Free Spending

I agree to think before I buy or to not spend at all.

To have true wealth and wisdom, you must be a conscious consumer. That means finding a reasonable way to enjoy the material things money buys without getting caught in a cycle of impulsive, compulsive overspending. When you balance your spending habits, you neither overly deprive yourself nor overly indulge in a momentary impulse. Maintaining a balance in your spending habits gives you control of your money, allowing you to make sound decisions about what you do or do not do with it; keep in mind that compulsive savers are just as out of balance as compulsive spenders.

Unlike addictions such as gambling and alcoholism, compulsive, impulsive spending is a legal, socially acceptable, and often encouraged addiction. In fact, many people joke about "shopaholics" who have the home shopping network numbers programmed into their speed dial and who run to the mall on every possible occasion. But the fact remains that the cycle of compulsive, impulsive spending can be very painful, both financially and emotionally. Some people use retail therapy to fill a void in their lives or to cover up their feelings of loneliness, inadequacy, or depression, among others. The dilemma is being conscious of these dynamics, so you will know when a purchase is appropriate.

~~~~~~~~~~~~~

Wallet Wisdom Lesson

Substance abuse is
substance abuse:
It makes no difference
what the substance is.
Money is just another substance.

~~~~~~~~~~~~~

Susan had a habit of buying and then returning and buying and returning, sometimes without even opening the bag once she got it home. This cycle repeated it self for years until her marriage and finances were in shambles. Without consciously being aware of it at the time, Susan was essentially a "bulimic" shopper, buying hoards of clothes and other personal items (bingeing), and then returning (purging) those very same items after feelings of guilt about her purchases set in. For Susan, shopping had become a means to an emotional high; unfortunately, the feeling was temporary, as the bills and her husband's frustrations mounted.

Pushed to the brink, Susan was forced to acknowledge the destructive nature of a problem that at first had seemed like harmless shopping. Susan's overspending often ended in regret, and undermined her self-respect. Her subconscious mind received a powerful, negative message: "I cannot be trusted with money."

~~~~~~~~~~~~~

Wallet Wisdom Lesson

Guilt is the gift
that keeps on giving
and giving and giving.

~~~~~~~~~~~~~

Once she recognized that she had a problem, Susan asked her husband for his support while she took concrete action to manage her "bulimic" money behaviors. The first of many important changes that

Susan made was to stop using shopping as a means of an emotional high and as a form of entertainment. Instead, she redirected her energies and began to volunteer her time at the local "Working Wardrobes" charity to help low-income women find suitable clothing for work.

The complexity of Susan's situation reveals that identifying the source of spending habits can be difficult. What complicates the matter even more is that money is the accepted means of trade. It is meant to be circulated in exchange for goods and services. In reality, there is little else that you do with money—even if you save it or invest it, at some point you likely plan to trade it for something you want or leave it to someone else who *will* spend it. So the "spending money" decision-making process becomes all the more important to attaining not only wealth, but the wisdom to use that wealth to your best advantage.

Determining your personal decision-making process is made more difficult because of the seduction and glitter all around, bombarding you from every quarter with assurances that money buys love, status, and approval. Take a moment to stop and observe the underlying concepts in the flurry of "buy" messages you encounter every day. Many products are even named for the emotions they are supposed to evoke. Car advertisements play on emotions just like most products. They appeal to a sense of speed, safety, or adventure, implying that you can have all these things only if you buy their product. Take a moment to consider which cars represent status and luxury. The next time you watch TV, listen to the radio, or flip through your favorite magazine, see how many products are named for emotions. The advertiser's job is to convince you that the only joy lies in buying their product, be it jewelry, fancy chocolates, or fast cars. The truth is, there is joy, delight, and excitement when such purchases are made—but only when they are made with conscious integrity.

Conscious consumers take time to think before thousands of daily "buy now" messages seduce them. Unfortunately, this can be difficult when you encounter an overwhelming number of messages telling you that the more you buy, the more you will save. Sale is a four-letter word designed to elicit an automatic response to buy now, lest the sale end and you miss the opportunity. The message seems to be that if you are willing to spend yourself into debt and financial oblivion, you can save even more money. Consider the emotions that advertisements appeal to in order to get you to buy certain products; it might prevent you from messing with your financial integrity to satisfy some unconscious need to acquire "stuff."

Merchandisers spend millions testing a product's placement, name, and packaging, in the hopes of getting you to choose their product over the many others that compete for your attention. The psychology of merchandising is that the most expensive shelf space in any store is eye level. You have to look either below or above for less known brands. What are merchandisers trying to accomplish by placing those items there? They want to attract your eye to the most expensive product, whether it is something you need, or not. Certainly, people with children realize the power and the problem of that colorful display of candy at the checkout.

Every store is laid out to encourage "Oh, by the way" purchases. The next time you walk into a store to purchase one or two items, pay attention to how many other things you buy (or are even tempted to buy) along the way to get what you originally intended to purchase. Count the number of sale or reduced-for-clearance signs you see. Once you become more aware of the merchandising tactics used to get you to buy, you can making conscious choices instead of responding to unconscious seduction.

Combine your newfound awareness of merchandising strategies with a few simple personal shopping guidelines to help you become more conscious of what and when you buy. A good way to get your spending under control is to read your vision statement often. In Lesson One of this book, you wrote a description of the life you desire. When considering a purchase, ask yourself if it fits this picture and whether it is based on your own unique value system or on someone else's notions of what will provide happiness.

The following guidelines will help you to begin the practice of thinking before you buy, thereby eliminating buyer's remorse, regret, and angst. Perhaps most importantly, you should remember that you have the courage and determination to control your money, rather than allowing your money to control you.

Make a shopping list for everything, not just groceries. For example, what pieces of clothing do you need this season? How much do you plan to spend?

Plan your shopping trips. If you are rushed, you are more likely to make impulsive purchases.

1. Go back and see the item a second time. If you feel you must have the item now, it is most likely a compulsive purchase.
2. Ask yourself any or all of the following questions:
    - Do I feel nurtured by this purchase?
    - What is the spirit behind this purchase?
    - Do I need ________________ to feel good about myself?
    - Am I using money to cover my depressed feelings?
    - Is this item in alignment with my personal integrity?
    - Does it fit with my vision for wealth?
    - Am I being a wise buyer or will I have buyer's remorse?

Until you get into the habit of being in integrity with yourself, you might want to carry the amount of cash you plan on spending, and leave your debit card, credit cards, and your checkbook in the car or at home. It may feel like you are on plastic deprivation for a short time, but the sensation is short lived. You can always go back and get them if you need to do so. Using paper money is different than using plastic because it is a tactile sensation. You can actually *see* and *feel* the transaction as it happens. Plastic is a concept. The reality of using actual dollars can be important step in helping you to gain control over your money.

While using shopping as a band-aid to cover and soothe emotional pain is unfortunately all too common; what is not common is an understanding that once this destructive behavior is under control, you may be left with an indescribable feeling of emptiness. A new sense of self-respect and money in the bank at the end of the month may combine with an almost-physical need to buy something, anything. It is helpful to recognize, understand, and honor these emotional pulls and pushes as a natural part of the process.

Feeling a general sense of emptiness is similar to the natural cycles found in nature. You anticipate seasonal changes and learn what to expect as summer blurs into fall—the leaves fall, the landscape loses its brilliance, cooler temperatures follow. Somehow in the spring, the flowers grow again in all their natural wonder. Everything has its season of growth and then retreat. The moon waxes and wanes; the ocean flows in during high tide and retreats at low tide. Arguing with nature's cycles or trying to change them to suit your needs is impossible. In the same way, human beings have cycles of high and low tides that are natural as the tides of the ocean.

Embracing the natural part of this cycle, your emotional low tide eases the root cause of unconscious spending. The low tide period provides you with the ability to fulfill your natural need to pause, rest, regroup, and regenerate. Some cultures embrace this human need for regeneration, weaving rituals such as the siesta or the practice of meditation into the fabric of everyday life. Western society does just the opposite. Often the need to take time out is ignored, and instead the drive to push forward at any cost is applauded. Our society prizes the businessperson who works a 60-hour week; it holds up as a hero the athlete who keeps on playing, in spite of an injury. The idea of letting go and relaxing into a natural low tide finds little support in American culture. Instead, the mantra is, "Do more, run more, buy more—have more and more and more". No matter how many things we buy, it will never be enough in the hectic, fast paced, push-ahead-at-all-costs society in which we live.

One way to hold back a personal low tide is overspending on yourself and others. The seduction of "buying happiness" is so overwhelming for many people that to buy something, anything, is the accepted way to avoid low tide feelings. Shopping is easy to do; it is socially and economically acceptable to follow the masses to the mall and be comforted by spending. Still, comfort spending does not sustain peace, wealth, or even long-term comfort. Love, understanding, and acceptance are not for sale at any store, no matter what you may have been led to believe. Catalogs do not keep compassion or joy in stock.

Listed below are several alternatives to consider, instead of thinking you can buy good feelings at the store. It is possible and highly satisfying to give gifts to yourself in nurturing ways. Notice the left-hand column below: Here is the catalog that stocks what we really want.

Peace	Take an early morning walk.
Appreciation	List ten things you do well.
Growth	Keep a victory journal.
Love	Contact a long-lost friend.
Contentment	Go to the library.
Luxury	Have breakfast in bed.
Connection	Let someone do you a favor.
Awe	Watch the sunset.
Creativity	Write a poem.
Lightness	Clean a closet.

Instead of overspending when you are feeling low, it is much wiser to give yourself a greater sense of safety and security by contributing to your own savings plan. However, the very word "savings" drives some people to distraction and, for many, is at best frustrating. Some people think they have failed to save enough or that they have used their savings in stupid ways. Most people have been taught to "save for a rainy day." On the surface, this seems like good advice, but saving only for a rainy day can become a self-fulfilling prophecy, a way of predicting that you *will have* some type of money problem or drama. You have no implied permission to withdraw the money, even if, by definition, it really is a "rainy day" such as being laid off or needing money for some unexpected event.

A savings plan gives you a sense of wealth, safety, and security that cannot be purchased by overspending. You might think of saving in the same way you would of starting a new exercise program. Call it the "savings muscle." You begin a physical exercise program by looking at yourself in a mirror and deciding what you will look like when you are really "buff." You start slowly, with smaller weights, and build up to a program that will produce the desired results. Look at your money situation and decide what your savings muscle will ultimately look like.

Start exercising your savings muscle slowly. To start, think about your savings plan in terms of percentages, instead of amounts. For example, if you have a monthly income of $4,000, you may want to start by saving 2% of your income.

$4,000 x 2% = $80.00
$4,000 – $80.00 (in savings) = $3,920.00 spending income

The significant number is $3,920. It is not too difficult to adjust your spending to live on $3,920 instead of $4,000. These calculations may seem small, but still add up to several hundred over the course of a year. Several hundred that would have been spent on guilt-producing items that you no longer even use. Remember you have just started the "extra money" exercise program. You don't develop washboard abdominal muscles or a flat stomach after the first week—but you will never have them if you never start. Likewise, if you decide to participate in an exercise program that requires you to walk for forty minutes a day, five days a week, you may start by walking for twenty minutes a day for the first week. Then, add ten minutes a day until you build up to the required time. The same is true for savings. When you are comfortable with your initial plan, bump up the percentage until you reach a level you can live with and which will produce the results you want to achieve. Many say that saving 10% of your income is an ideal amount to strive for, but you must decide what is best for you and your situation.

After you've developed an effective savings plan, develop a fun and detailed plan that outlines how you will use extra, unexpected money. By planning for extra money, you make it emotionally safe to receive a windfall, inheritance, bonus, or extra money from any source. The following exercise is designed to help you be creative with your money. Even if you do not have lots of money right now, play along and have some fun with this exercise.

List five or six things for which you would spend the money you are setting aside. Because the amount you will ultimately accumulate is unknown at this time, use percentages of money, but do not go over 100%. The categories will come from your situation. The following are merely examples:

Vacation	Clothes
Debt Reduction	Savings
Home Remodeling	Furniture

This exercise is to determine categories and the percentage of money you would spend on each category. Here is an example of the percentages of distribution:

Category	Person A	Person B
Vacation	10%	25%
Debt	25%	10%
Furniture	20%	10%
Clothes	20%	5%
Savings	20%	15%
Remodeling	5%	35%

In this example, it is easy to see that each person had different values and places different priorities on how to use the money. Assuming this example represents a couple, the next step is to spend time negotiating these percentages so they reach an agreement, or at least a livable compromise. Neither person may get exactly what they want, but each would have a say in how the money is spent.

Years of overspending, retail therapy, shame, and anxiety may cause you to have a love-hate relationship with money. You may subconsciously think that extra money would only mean more dramatic problems, but when you plan ahead, two things happen. First, you begin to imagine a life beyond struggle, and second, a plan gives your money a purpose before it arrives and helps to reduce fears of over-spending. Amy's situation illustrates the importance of planning ahead.

Amy was due to inherit a significant amount of money from a person she worked for, but she initially did not feel she deserved the money because she had not earned it. What's more, because she had a tendency to overspend, she feared she would, in her words, "go crazy" with the money given to her. Amy counteracted her fear of overspending by making a plan for the extra money that included real estate investments. She was able to accept the money gracefully and with peace, because she knew ahead of time what she was going to do with it.

Understanding the hidden spending motivation is a process that can take some time. Be patient with yourself as you may slip and slide a bit. Remember to use your vision statement as a guidepost when considering what and when to buy. Then appreciate and enjoy the blessings of your abundance with peace and gratitude for your personal financial integrity.

Chapter

5 Money, the Last Taboo

I agree to communicate openly and honestly with myself and others.

Being open and honest about money with others and ourselves often is difficult because talking openly about money is one of our culture's last great taboos. We readily discuss a wide range of topics including sex and politics, but from an early age we learn it is considered impolite to talk about money. Most companies, in fact, keep salaries a secret for fear that knowing what others earn would cause discord among the staff. Few people discuss money even with their family or closest friends. While we may know the most intimate personal details of each other's lives, in all likelihood, we know little or nothing about the financial lives of those closest to us.

Learning to communicate openly and honestly means learning to recognize the number one assumption that confuses communication about money: the idea that everyone thinks and talks about money in the same way you do. We all learn to communicate about money in a way that is uniquely our own, though it often is result of our upbringing and attitudes. One way to prevent financial misunderstandings is to avoid talking in generalities. For example, what does "Let's not spend too much money" mean? Or for that matter, how about "I can't afford it," or "I don't have any money"? A top-rated movie star's "can't afford it" means something different than when a middle manager supporting a spouse and four children says the same thing.

The point is that the words you use about money do not necessarily mean the same thing to everybody. If somebody says, "I don't have any money," part of learning to communicate openly requires that you ask more questions. In doing so, you might be surprised to find how widely your ideas vary. Does "no money" mean there is no food for the week and gas in the car? Does it mean liquid assets are tied up, or does it mean that person would rather not move money from one account to another? In terms of money, even the most seemingly simple words can mean different things to different people, as was the case when Robert met a new acquaintance for dinner. He thought he was being open and honest when he said, "I don't want to go to an expensive restaurant." His companion responded by saying, "What do you call expensive?" This seemed like an obvious question, but one that was very unsettling for Robert. He didn't want to sound like a cheapskate or hard up for money, but he didn't want it to appear as if he was extravagant either. Robert suddenly became aware of the vast amount of interior dialog he went through simply to clearly define an "expensive" restaurant.

We often take for granted that we agree on the meaning of many concepts, including the situation that Robert faced when deciding where to have dinner. Just as you are likely to have your own definition of what constitutes an expensive restaurant, so you have your own ideas about what is meant by terms such as *financial success, freedom, security, and independence*. One person's definition of financial freedom might mean saying no to work they do not want to do, while another person's idea of financial freedom might be working part time. How would you define financial freedom or financial success? Have you ever taken time to define these money ideals for yourself? Communicating honestly with yourself is only possible when you clarify the direction of your own money game.

~~~~~~~~~~~~~

Wallet Wisdom Lesson

The ability to say NO
is the power to say YES.

~~~~~~~~~~~~~

Before you can have truthful communications with others, you have to learn the lesson of being honest with yourself. Presenting a pretty picture to other people by acting and sounding as if you have it all together is the opposite of wealth. Do you put on an all too common "everything is perfect" false posture about money? Are you pretending that you know just how to handle money, that you have lots of it, that you are doing everything exactly right and have never made a financial mistake? Or perhaps you may know people who act like this, but really are being dishonest with themselves and others.

Boasting, posturing, and being a financial *know-it-all* are simply ways to hide the truth. The people doing the boosting may not realize they're being dishonest with themselves; but typically this behavior covers up a deep insecurity about money. The unexpected aspect of denial is that people are not aware that they are in denial. That is why it is called denial. Their unconsciously dishonest communication covers up a truth that seems too scary to address. It's easier for them to pretend, make excuses, or to just avoid the subject entirely. Getting kicked out of denial usually involves a wake-up call in the form of stressful or negative feedback or circumstances that demand immediate attention and action. The emotional pain that results is often just what is needed to get past the cover-up and learn the lesson of the power of honesty in relationship to money.

While denial and co-dependency are words not usually associated with money, they do in fact describe many peoples' self-destructive behavior. Financial co-dependency is where one person denies their needs and desires to take care of others or pretends to look prosperous to their friends and family. Denying one's own needs to take care of the financial needs of the others is another form of dishonesty. The only thing it does is to ensure impoverished relationships with those you've over-helped. Remember the last time you were on an airplane and the flight attendant performed the safety demonstration? The flight attendant reminded you that if you were flying with a small child, you should put on your own oxygen mask before helping the child. For most people, their natural tendency is to help their child first. Of course, the problem is that if you are not breathing, you cannot possibly save the child. The same principle applies to money. If you are not financially "breathing," how can you help others?

~~~~~~~~~~~~~

Wallet Wisdom Lesson

Put on your own financial oxygen mask
then give to others
from your abundance.

~~~~~~~~~~~~~

People who pick up the lunch tab for everyone even if they don't have money to pay their monthly bills are practicing one form of denial. Another form is the habit of buying things just to be like everyone else or have the latest and greatest whatever. The types of people who practice these behaviors have deeper personal insecurities that often translate into denial regarding money matters. As you become honest with yourself, the related insecurities will begin to diminish and will be replaced with self-respect, integrity, and wealth.

One way to be honest with yourself is to develop a set of out-of-bounds behavior rules that brings you a deeper sense of internal financial security. Are you willing to ask yourself probing questions before you say "yes?" Are you willing to keep a money diary that tracks your spending patterns? Will you institute a "waiting period" for purchases over a certain dollar amount? Is it okay to pay high interest to obtain something you want now?

Once you develop a set of out-of-bounds behaviors for yourself, communicating honestly with others happens more easily. Doing so will help you avoid many complicated financial situations, because money usually involves other people. The root cause of these behaviors typically has nothing to do with money. People often have a hidden agenda for excessive giving. If you constantly over give, you may have an unconscious need to control the situation, buy love, or give your life meaning and purpose by having other people depend on you. It is easy to fall into this trap—all of us want to be loved, needed, and appreciated. As a result, money can serve as convenient way to manipulate and control, while making it seem as though you are being kind and generous. So take a deep look inside and get honest with yourself regarding your motivation in giving and giving and giving—as Diana did when she found herself in a large department store.

For the longest time, Diana could not think of a thing she wanted for herself. She could think of dozens of things to buy for her friends, her grandchild, and especially her grown children, but typically did not consider buying anything for herself. Despite Diana's inclination to spend money on her children, they were quite capable financially and felt embarrassed by her overspending on things they did not need her to buy.

After discussing her spending habits honestly, Diana realized that she found purpose in pretending that her children still needed her financially, as if they were still little kids and Diana were still a young mother. She decided that it was time for her to get on with her life, and accordingly, began to say "yes" to herself by focusing on her own dreams and visions. The challenge for Diana was to accept that her work as a mother was finished and that she deserved to have the things she longed to have.

Knowing how to distinguish between when you are telling yourself the truth or when you are using money to control or buy love is a wisdom lesson. You may find that making these distinctions is not always the easiest thing to do when the occasion arises, but with a continued commitment, you will take this lesson to heart. A useful habit is to silently question your behaviors before you take action, realizing that each situation is different. You can pick from one or more of the questions given below, incorporating them in your open and honest communications with yourself and others.

- Is this a reasonable and financially rational thing for me to do?
- Is this an appropriate way for me to spend my money?
- What else do I need to know before I say "yes" to this?
- What other expenses do I have that I might have forgotten about?
- Have I planned for this month's necessary items?

Because you will be talking honestly with other people about money, make it a practice to ask questions then rather than to make assumptions. Adopt one or more of the following statements before you get into a situation that has the potential for financial pitfalls.

- Let me think about that.
- I need more details about the costs.

- What do you mean by ___________?
- Are we going Dutch or what?
- How will we decide how to pay for this ___________?

The more honest you are with others, the more implied permission they have to be honest with you. When you are willing to raise your standards of honest communications while maintaining your personal dignity and self-respect, then other people will likely do the same. People tend to feel safer talking with people who are honest with them. You might be surprised at some of the wonderful things that happen as a result of your clear, concise communications.

- Tell me about what it will cost to do ___________?
- I don't know yet if _________ is a wise thing for me to do right now.
- That's more than I want to spend right now.
- I can spend between ___________ and ___________.

Honest money conversations tend to be even more sensitive when dealing with close personal relationships—be it with your boyfriend/girlfriend, spouse, or child.

This point was illustrated in a single evening when over one hundred singles attended a money management seminar. Among the many topics of discussion was who pays for what on a date. Remember, the rule that a man pays for everything is no longer the case for most young people. One young man in his early thirties insisted that a woman must offer to pay for dinner by the third date. If she did not offer, he would not call her again. However, if she did offer, he noted he was not likely to accept money from her anyway. When questioned as to whether he would tell the woman what he expected and why, he replied, "No, I want her to offer on her own."

He essentially believed a woman should read his mind, and if she did not, he would not ask her out again. The woman would probably not understand what she had done wrong, and even if she somehow figured out that she was supposed to offer to pay, he still would have rejected her offer. Further discussion revealed that he wanted to be sure he was not being taken for granted and that he really wasn't interested in the money or who paid for the date. For this man, the offer symbolized an equal partnership. While there is nothing wrong with striving for equality in a relationship, his lack of communication probably will keep him single for a long time to come. It is virtually impossible to build a solid relationship foundation by guessing what someone expects of you financially.

~~~~~~~~~~~~~

Wallet Wisdom Lesson

Money problems are a convenient mask to avoid intimacy.

~~~~~~~~~~~~~

It is wise to decide the money ground rules ahead of time in a relationship. Some couples discuss each situation when it comes up. For example, if you are planning to go away for the weekend, do you know what your partner expects of you financially? Are you guessing and will you then be surprised when the bill arrives and you hadn't planned on paying for a particular item? The sooner you talk honestly about expenses, the easier it will be to make those romantic plans. Are you splitting everything, or is the weekend one person's treat? The best time to find out is *before* the trip.

One married couple found out why open and honest pre-planning communications are important when they went on a weekend mini-vacation. While at the hotel, Laurie had a complete spa treatment. She assumed Brian would want to treat her to this luxury as part of the trip, but when the bill arrived, he presented it to Laurie. Brian felt Laurie was being unreasonable, and she felt he didn't appreciate her. The sad part is that neither person was necessarily right or wrong, and regardless of how they ultimately resolved the situation, both people suffered because of a breakdown in pre-planning financial communication.

Poor communication about money can be a troubling issue for couples, so troubling in fact, that money is among the top three stated reasons for getting a divorce. Avoiding honest financial communications is not an option if you are committed to having wealth and wisdom. Men and women generally have different communications styles. Developing your expertise in money communications is easier when you realize that women tend to be more verbal, talking things out until they figure out what to do and then following the discussion with action. On the other hand, men generally say very little until they figure out what their next move is going to be. Once they know how they will proceed, then they talk about it. Add the sensitive subject of money to the gender communications mix and it is easy to understand that what one partner says is not necessarily the same thing the other partner hears. Stir in the emotional investment in the relationship as well as real or imagined fears about being shamed or criticized, and you have a recipe for disaster.

The following Wealthy U Meeting Guidelines were designed to help make financial communications more harmonious and productive among significant others or even in a business situation. These guidelines are based on the same idea as a money discussion in a business meeting. Think of your "money meeting" as a "business meeting" for your relationship. Emotion and unclear communication have no place in a business meeting. Please remember to keep in mind that clear, honest money communication is an on-going process.

Action Item—Wealthy U Money Meeting

For the purposes of this Action Item, think of your money meeting the same way you would think of any other sport or game. As in every game, including the "Money Game," there is a set of rules and regulations by which to play. Prior to the first meeting, discuss and agree on definitions of such common words as, *financial success, freedom, security, and independence*. Each partner gets to pick the word or words that best describe their personal notion of wealth and wisdom. Just remember, million-dollar football players know the technique of their game and its boundaries before they go on the playing field. When you finish answering the questions, ask your spouse/significant other or any other person with whom you co-mingle money to do the same. When both of you are finished, compare answers. Where are your answers similar? Where are your differences? What can be negotiated? Use the example below as a way to get started. At the top of the page, write the following sentence:

I am financially ____________ (fill in the word from the paragraph above that best describes what you want). Then list your criteria for the term you use to fill in the blank. An example of your list might be:

I am financially successful.

- I pay all of my obligations in full and on time.
- I own my home.
- I can buy what I want and pay for it with cash.
- I give generously to my favorite charities.
- I have a prosperous investment portfolio.

What else can you add to your list? Add to your list as you think of things that define financial success for you. You may wish to gather pictures and put them in the notebook along with your written description of success, or you may have already done this as part of your vision statement. You will want to do this exercise jointly with the person with whom you are building wealth and wisdom. Just imagine the wonderful, intimate wealth conversation that will result from open and honest communications beyond the everyday tasks.

When you finish defining the terms pertinent to your Wealth Game, the next step is to determine the how the Wealth Game is played. You can do this by answering the following questions individually and with your partner.

1. What is the object of our Wealth Game?

____

____

____

____

____

2. What is our game plan for achieving the object of the game?

3. Where are the goal posts? Which financial behaviors are "out of bounds?"

4. How will we settle disputes?

Once you establish the foundation for your money communications, you are ready to discuss the ground rules for your regularly scheduled money meetings. You may want to consider some of the following as out-of bounds behaviors: no raised voices, a ten-minute time out when there are disagreements, no complaining or blaming each other, et cetera. What other agreements can you establish to conduct your own money meeting?

Some guidelines to consider:

- Always set aside a specific time to meet, and meet on a consistent basis. It is best to meet weekly for at least the first six months.
- Have a starting time and an ending time. No more than one hour is recommended.
- If possible, meet in a neutral territory such as a park or favorite restaurant to eliminate potential interruptions such as the telephone or children.
- Have an agenda for the meeting to discuss such topics as reviewing bills or planning for the next month or unexpected expenses.
- Bring paper and pen/pencil so you can record whatever you have decided for later review. This will ensure each person understands what is going to happen.
- It is recommended that you keep an ongoing record of these meetings, allowing for new ground to be covered each time rather than going over the same issues again and again. Keep your agreements in a place where you can find them, such as on your computer or in binder notebook. The topics of your money meetings are great wealth reference material in the months and years to come as your chart your wealth course. You can create your own recording format, or you may want to use something like the one given below. Your "Money Logbook" is a written record of the decisions reached at each meeting.

OUR WEALTHY U's MONEY LOG BOOK

Date	Agenda Item	Outcomes/Decisions
Action Plan for Week of ____________________		

Remember, conventional financial wisdom may not be the best choice for your particular situation. For example, many married couples have one joint checking account. This may have worked well when one person was at home and the checkbook stayed put. Today, we live in a fast-paced, mobile society where both people often work outside the home. Having to remember to debit a check at a later time can become a set-up for failure. Similarly, remembering to enter an ATM withdrawal or who wrote what check at what store when the checkbook is not available may lead to unnecessary arguments. Even electronic bill paying services or statement downloading needs to be checked once in a while. There are no hard and fast rules about what system will work best for your situation as a couple. The important thing is to recognize that your parent's or friend's system may not work for you. In every relationship, merging at least some money makes sense. It symbolizes working together as a couple to achieve shared goals and dreams. Having only a "his and hers" system would tend to indicate a lack of trust in each other or fear of merging your lives. You may decide to change your system as you experiment and find out what works for you and discover what, if any, holes there are in your system. Money is a complex subject and the least romantic thing to discuss. Setting up a system that works for you with the understanding and acceptance of a common philosophy, goals, and priorities may help the longevity of romance.

But just as you learned your money management behavior from your parents and other family members, your children will learn from you. The example you set with your honest communications, your attitudes, and methods for handling money will spill over to your children's behavior. Parents have the complicated task of teaching their children about money, a task made more complex by the fact that we are in the second and third generation of bank card users and abusers. Children often see their parents use plastic to get them what they want, and best of all, plastic gets it right now! On the flip side, they rarely see or relate to the bills that follow. For children, the concept of cause and effect becomes difficult to understand. Randy was witness to this when he taught his seven-year-old son his ATM code. When Randy told his child "no" when he asked for something, the child's solution was to tell his dad to go the machine and get some more money. In this child's young mind and experience, the ATM generates the money with no limitations.

Many parents simply are unconscious of what and how they communicate with their children. One area of difficulty is broken agreements between parent and child. A child asks for something such as a bike or some other large ticket item. The parent says, "If you earn, save, or contribute part of the money, then I will pay for the rest." The child does what is required of them. Then, for whatever reason, the child either does not get what is promised, or the parent changes the deal. With this "bait and switch" tactic, a child picks up a no-win attitude about money. They may even conclude that it is "dumb" to work for what they want because they don't get it anyhow.

Another way parents may have a long-term affect on their child's ability to manage money is to be overly controlling with what their child earns. Jason began working at fifteen because he wanted to have extra money for things that his father would typically not purchase. Instead of getting to buy things a teenager would want, he had to pay rent to his father with the money he made. When he became an adult and was able to leave home, he went totally out of control with money, spending himself into debt and distress. Children will often go to the opposite financial extreme of their parents, especially if money was used to control them.

It is just as detrimental to overindulge adult children who are capable of taking care of themselves. Some parents are tempted to buy their child's love, some may be feeding their own guilt because they are too busy to spend time with their child, or it may be that they want to give their children everything they did not have. This was the case for a couple that was in distress over their daughter's choice to attend an expensive out-of-state college. They anguished over the fact that they could not qualify to co-sign her large student loans. Despite the fact that they were unable to help her attend the more expensive college, she had been granted a scholarship to a local state school. The most logical school seemed obvious, but these parents tortured themselves with guilt instead of telling themselves and their daughter the truth about their financial circumstances. Being honest from the start with their daughter would have saved them the anguish they felt, and it also would have been a positive behavior for their daughter to model. Additionally, it would give her the gift of being debt-free after college, rather than being obligated to repay thousands of dollars in student loan payments.

Determining when and why to give to children is something that parents need to work out together. Compassion and understanding and even financial support are sometimes called for when grown children are between jobs or have other unusual circumstances. However, the time comes when such giving is counterproductive. Once the parent of an adult child reaches the point where giving is counterproductive (which is different for each situation), they may want to establish a transition period. Decide upon a grace period of "x" number days or months that you will support the child as agreed. If, for example, you decide that you will not pay your child's car insurance after the first of the year, be prepared to let them pay the consequences for non-payment. Telling the truth by keeping your word is the most productive money lesson a parent can teach.

There usually is not an optimum cutoff date for closing the "Bank of Mom and Dad"; it depends upon the family situation. Temporary hardships may mean the bank stays open a bit longer. Before you make decisions, take time to talk with each other openly and honestly and work out a plan that is beneficial and acceptable to both parents and for your adult child. Both you and your child may need to compromise to reach a joint decision. Just because a child demands an answer right now does not mean you must not say you and your significant other need some time to work out a plan.

Honest communications are even more complex for children of divorced parents. Divorced parents can reduce the effect of mixed money messages by working out agreements ahead of time about what to teach their children regarding borrowing and spending money. This may be a monumental task if money problems led to the divorce in the first place. It also can become a problem if the child lives with one parent who provides a majority of the child's basic needs. Sometimes when the child visits the other parent, he or she receives extravagant gifts. The child quickly learns how to play parents against each other. Divorced parents have more than one family's money values to consider in order before they can be honest and open with their child about financial matters. The following Action Item expands the couples' money meeting to include children in open and honest communications.

Action Item—Children's Money Meeting

Include children in money meetings just as soon as they can understand a TV commercial. It is never too early to begin explaining simple money concepts.

Make reasonable money arrangements with children and honor them. If they are old enough, have them write down these agreements in their own words to make sure they understand what has been decided. If not, have them repeat back to you what they heard.

Talk with other parents, especially friends of your child, when you hear the words "everyone has one." Ask them if they really are planning to buy that expensive "whatever" to determine if your child is telling you the whole story. Design a level playing field for children, using the same sports game format as for adult money meetings.

- What behaviors are out of bounds?
- What is the objective of the Money Game?
- What are the rules of the game?
- How do you win with money?

Simple answers for teaching your children about money do not exist. However, the first place to look is to your own behaviors. What changes must you make within yourself to live a richly fulfilled and joyously prosperous lifestyle? What financial behaviors do you want pass onto your children?

Being open and honest with yourself and others is a good practice in general. Your communications about money often indicates how you relate to money, and the way you behave with money is generally the way you behave in your life. If you are secretive and tight with money, you are most likely just as secretive and tight emotionally. The irresponsible person who pretends to have lots of money or spends money to impress is very likely an individual who is generally not being honest with others about anything else in their life either. When you are open and honest with yourself and others, you begin to gain self-confidence and self-trust.

Chapter 6

Woulda, Coulda, Shoulda

I agree to trust myself to make reasonable and rational financial decisions.

Lurking somewhere inside of you is the critic who has tremendous power if you allow it unfettered control over your money decisions. Sometimes called "the committee," your internal critic is the nagging and persistent voice that constantly calls into question your ability to make reasonable and rational financial decisions. It is sometimes difficult to identify your inner critic because it has been a part of you for long time. The self-talk dialogue you hear has been an accepted part of your everyday thought process. No matter what you call your internal critic, identifying, grappling with, and taming Mr. Critic is a big part of establishing the wisdom to have wealth.

Your internal critic is very good at causing you to second guess your ability to make wise financial decisions. It accomplishes this through a constant barrage of varied negative messages. It tells you that mistakes are not acceptable, it reminds you of past failures, and it convinces you that you are destined to make the same mistakes and fail again. Mr. Critic demands that you must know everything there is to know about finances, and above all, it promises that you will never get it right.

Your internal critic works on a number of different levels, but its main joy is to effectively induce you to maintain the status quo. Mr. Critic warns you that making a change could set you up for failure and so coaxes you into doing nothing. Mr. Critic operates best on the fear of the unknown, where imagined failures live. Rather than risk, Mr. Critic causes you to second-guess your financial decisions, keeping you trapped in a cycle of fear. Your internal critic prevents you from trusting yourself to have vast amounts of money. Mr. Critic reasons that if you do not have large amounts of money, you will never have to fear making even bigger mistakes. Giving power to the internal critic appears to keep you safe and comfortable, but Mr. Critic really will keep you poor.

Your internal critic also works diligently to ensure that you do not forget past errors. If you have ever blown it with a losing investment or thought that you spent money unwisely, then Mr. Critic has more ammunition to continually remind you of the mistakes. It is that inner voice that echoes with "should," "ought to" and "have to," mixed together with some "if only" that might sound something like, "If only I knew then what I know now, then I would have not made that stupid mistake." Mr. Critic tells you that you could easily make an unwise decision again and again.

Your internal critic does not operate in a vacuum as he drains energy and undermines your self-confidence. Doom and gloom headlines are all around, promising a recession or a plummeting stock market. Voices of authority (economists, financial analysts, and others) say things that make the average person lose confidence in their decisions. When you hear and see money fears expressed everywhere around you, it takes courage and resolve to be your own authority figure.

Listening carefully for the echoing internal critic's bad news chorus that second-guesses your financial decisions begins to drain its power. In its place will come self-respect, self-confidence, and belief in your ability to be wealthy and wise. Access your personal internal wisdom by developing a strong, assertive financial backbone. Being assertive means identifying your needs and taking action.

The process of developing a strong financial backbone is different for everyone, depending on your financial situation. One way to do this is to ask more questions before you make a financial decision. What do you really need to know before you decide, and are there other ways to accomplish the same objective? In a temporary money crunch, Bill found himself needing to develop his financial backbone when his clients were taking a long time to pay him for services he provided. Because he was operating on a low cash reserve due to several recent business reverses, his clients' slow pay impacted his ability to pay his own bills on time. One creditor informed him he must pay before a certain date or he would be penalized. Normally, paying his bills on time was not an issue for Bill, but right now he was feeling the domino effects of his clients taking their time to pay him. In order to pay one creditor, he was faced with deciding to use his small reserves, or waiting until he was paid. He knew he would soon have additional funds, but did not know exactly when they would arrive. His first thought was to stretch himself financially and satisfy the creditor's time requirements.

He wondered over and over again if that was the best decision. If only his clients would pay on time then he would not have this dilemma. His internal critic took over, giving him sleepless nights and questioning him about what he was doing wrong. Bill's internal critic was actively diverting his productive energy while he tried to figure out how to get paid on time, satisfy the creditor's demands, and stay focused on building his business. Mustering his confidence, he personally called some of his long-time clients and asked about the status of their payment. Once he had this information he called his creditor to explain his situation. He asked for an extension, due to his unusual situation at the moment. His consistent payment record showed his integrity in the matter, and his creditor agreed to the extension he proposed. The immediate financial crunch gave Bill's critic ammunition to feed his emotional and financial distress, but he decided to ignore Mr. Critic and move into action, using the situation to build his financial backbone. He asked his clients direct questions before making a decision and developed a new payment policy for his business so the situation would not happen again.

When the internal critic voice was the loudest, he began to resent his clients for taking advantage of his good nature. He heard lots of mind chatter, including Mr. Critic telling him, "You're a real screw-up." Once he recognized where the chatter was coming from, he was able to laugh and tell Mr. Critic to take the day off. Bill was able to get down to the business of closing deals and making more money, recognizing that there were reasonable and rational actions steps he could take.

Bill used powerful words to help him make a reasonable and rational financial decision. He said to himself and others, "Let me think about that overnight," or "I will get back to you." Bill got his emotional need to satisfy everyone's demands under control as he reviewed the best options and took all available time to make a rational money decision. Money decisions made in the heat of the moment usually lead to regret, giving your internal critic plenty of new material to use against you, as was the case for Joan.

~~~~~~~~~~~~~

Wallet Wisdom Lesson

Anger and hurt come from
self-betrayal of our souls,
our values, and
our value as human beings.

~~~~~~~~~~~~~

For Joan, every grocery store aisle seemed to echo with "I want" or "All the other kids have one." Tired of her children nagging her when they went shopping and knowing rationally how much money she had to spend, she decided to allow her children to choose one treat to take home. However, when she got to the store, they pleaded for this and for that. Caught in the immediacy of the moment, she caved. As her children toted new toys and enough junk food to keep them going all week, Joan felt drained and powerless to control her financial destiny. She was convinced that she had no financial sense, would never be a good mother, and just could not control her money. Her internal critic accompanied her all the way home. When was she going to ever going to learn? Who is in charge? Her, or her children? What was her husband going to say?

Joan arrived home feeling depressed. Upon reviewing the grocery bill and seeing the children lug in their loot, Joan's husband Paul reflected on his own experiences with their children at the store. He suggested a reasonable and rational solution that tamed the internal critic for both of them. One parent would go to the grocery store and the other would stay home with the kids until they felt more confident about their ability to make reasonable and rational financial decisions with their kids at the store. Joan and Paul began to develop their financial backbone by finding a solution that worked for them at the time. There may be a time when they feel confident enough to take the kids to the store and teach their children some powerful money lessons. Until that time arrives, they found the best answer for them.

Another strategy for improving your ability to make reasonable and rational financial decisions is to stand up for your financial rights, escalating a financial dispute if you need to do so. If some type of institutional mess has caused you a problem, do not stop until it's resolved. The escalator technique is a plan by which you determine the best way to resolve a problem, before you even begin the resolution process. Your escalator plan might follow this format: If I talk to person "A" and don't get a satisfactory answer, then I will talk to "B," and it that doesn't work, then I will write a letter to "C." An example of the escalator technique is illustrated in Rachelle's situation.

Rachelle, a newly certified teacher, had not received a paycheck in two months because her teaching certificate was lost somewhere in the state capitol. The local school district would not issue a paycheck until her teaching certificate was in their files. She had made several calls to the state capitol and got the bureaucratic run around. Her lack of a financial backbone was causing Rachelle a great deal of stress. Besides affecting her ability to pay her bills, she was losing her focus on teaching and was beginning doubt her decision to become a teacher.

She decided to forgo any more phone calls and instead began writing letters to the various agencies involved. She also contacted her state representative and the head of the state legislature's school committee. Within seventy-two hours of contacting her congressperson, Rachelle had her teaching certificate on file and a check in her hand. Rachelle refocused her attention on teaching and regained trust in herself and her newly developed financial backbone.

You can choose to accept a "no" from someone in authority if you think it is reasonable, but "the escalator technique" puts the control and power back into your hands. No matter the situation, if you do not receive a satisfactory answer to your questions or concerns, escalate your problem as far up the chain of command as you need to get the answer you expect. The key to your success is to ask more questions when you are not receiving a satisfactory resolution of the matter. Be polite, yet firm with the people to whom you are talking. If the first person you speak with is uncooperative, do not be afraid to ask to talk to the supervisor and so on up the chain of command until you get the answer you need. Trust yourself to use your own wisdom while developing your financial backbone.

By being assertive and paying attention to details, you stand to gain not only in financial health, but wealth and wisdom. Imagine finding an extra charge, say $10, on a bill. You may find it silly to challenge a $10 fee by sending a certified return-receipt letter to the company. Why not just pay the $10 and be done with it as millions of other people do each day? It makes sense to dispute the fee when you consider the significance of building trust with yourself to have tremendous amounts of money. Building self-trust begins with taking care of smaller amounts of money; it is a symbolic gesture of trusting yourself to deal with the bigger issues and amounts. You can make a practice of behaving as if you were already wealthy by not tolerating unwarranted charges that appear on your bills, no matter how small the amount. Your confidence with money and your wisdom grows and makes it easier to receive and handle vast sums of money.

Learning to trust your ability to make reasonable and rational financial decisions is a matter of appreciating small consistent action steps and giving yourself positive validation for positive changes. Make a note of any and all positive behavior changes. You may even want to keep a "Taming Mr. Critic" journal in which you record your positive money decisions and the changes you made to accomplish your results.

The process of changing internal critic self-talk into self-trust takes time and vigilant awareness. This process usually falls into three distinct phases. You do not usually experience change as a linear process as described in these phases. Rather, the process of changing your thinking seems like conscious peaks and unconscious valleys. As you become more conscious, you will spend less time reacting to negative behaviors after the fact when you are powerless to do anything about it. The first phase is to become more aware of counter-productive behavior that saps self-trust before anything actually happens.

After some practice, you will begin to notice your negative actions, behaviors, or patterns more quickly, or even more likely, while you are doing them. This can be a most frightening place to be on the journey of change into a wealthy person. Even though you realize that what you are doing is not in your best financial interests, you do it anyhow. It is like eating too much chocolate and, while you are in the act of eating it, saying to yourself "I should know better. I have to lose weight. This will make me fat," but you keep eating the chocolate instead of throwing it away. You may say yes to a friend's request for a temporary loan when you already know this person will not pay you back. You know you are setting yourself up to lose, but you loan the money anyhow. You may make wishy-washy financial agreements, knowing from past experience you are setting yourself up to lose, yet you feel powerless to do anything differently.

The dubious prize of consciousness is to be aware that what you are doing is counterproductive, but to continue doing it anyhow. It seems like you have given Mr. Critic new material with which to prove that you are hopeless. It may at times seem that he is right, but the process of change is similar to a six-hour road trip. You started the journey with eager anticipation. After about four hours on the road, the scenery has grown dull, and it seems like you'll never get there. You may say to yourself "I should have stayed home," "This is boring," "I could be doing a hundred other things," or "Why did I think this could be fun?" However, if you keep on keeping on to your destination, the trip begins to feel easier as you are seeing signs that let you know you are getting closer to where you want to be. Even though you are still not quite to your destination. It would not make sense to turn around and give up the journey just because you are temporarily stuck in traffic.

By phase two of the change process, you are making better decisions and the internal critic voice has grown quiet for the most part. Then, out of nowhere, you get a notion to do or buy something that will take you off track. You already know the mall is a dangerous place for you to be when you are feeling low. You've made great progress, having told all your friends that shopping is no longer your primary form of entertainment and finding out that they are still your friends. You have even found some other financially nurturing, fun activities. You're feeling like a champ, well on the way to wealth and wisdom. Yet on this particular day, somehow the car "drives itself" to the mall. Without even thinking about it, you are out of integrity with yourself again.

Mr. Critic jumps in and tells you to simply give up because you will never change. This is the most uncomfortable place in the process of change. At this point, your internal critic still has the power to control your self-trust, but you are really changing even if feels like you are very vulnerable during this process.

There are some similarities between what you are going through and a lobster going through its growth process. Can you imagine a lobster in a vulnerable, soft skin phase? This visual image demonstrates how vulnerable humans are as they change. Remember a lobster grows a hard skin, molts, changes form, and even colors as it grows to maturity. See if you can find the similarities between a lobster lifecycle and building your own self-trust.

How does a lobster grow bigger (change) when its shell is so hard? The only way is for a lobster to shed its shell at regular intervals. When its body begins to feel cramped inside the shell, the lobster instinctively looks for a reasonably safe spot to rest while the hard shell comes off and the pink membrane just inside forms the basis of the next shell. But no matter where a lobster goes for this shedding process, it is very vulnerable. It can get tossed against a coral reef or eaten by a fish. In other words, a lobster has to risk its life in order to grow.

Persistence and determination are key elements in silencing Mr. Critic during this phase of the change process. Building self-trust makes it possible for you to have wealth and wisdom faster than any other investment you can make in yourself. As you go through this vulnerable stage of change, it is important to be gentle with yourself. Take time to do something nice for yourself that rewards your progress. Continuing to keep your journal or notebook can be a useful tool to help you recognize your behaviors without judging yourself. Stick with it! You are making progress.

Rather than deal with the vulnerable part of change, some people snap back into their old shells of self-destructive, unconscious financial habits and beliefs. They seem to seem to prefer self-sabotage in order to stay safe, stuck within the known misery rather than struggling to reach a heretofore unknown potential happiness. Struggling and effort are so familiar they find it difficult to break the shell and move into being wealthy. Being consciously aware of the distinct phases in the process of change makes it much easier to trust yourself to make reasonable and rational financial decisions.

After some more practice with heightening your awareness and understanding the slips and backpedaling that sometimes happen when changing your behavior, you will enter phase three being more proactive, noticing actions before you do financial harm. Your physical body may begin giving you signals like a knot in the pit of your stomach, tense shoulders, or a tight chest as warning signs. As you trust yourself, you will learn to trust these intuitive signals. Your mind also will give early warning signs that the action you are about to take is not in your best interest. These intuitive signals may be mental messages or a sense that tells you to think before acting. The internal intuitive voice is different than the internal critic voice. It is usually quieter, not in a big hurry to act, and gently urges you ask more questions. It might say or sense something like, "Do you really want to do this right now?" or "Does this decision make sense?" It takes practice to distinguish between your intuition and the critic's voice. The best way to make the distinction is to get quiet and check within yourself by noticing body/mind signals and using them to make the wisest choices for you at the time. Trusting your gut feeling, along with having a written vision statement to give you direction and focus and sufficient information on which to base your decision elevates you to become wealthy.

Action Item—The Wealthy U Journal

Answer the following questions at the beginning of each month; make it a ritual to answer these questions each month to track your wealth building. After answering these questions, write down the positive change to which you will commit for that month.

The process of financial change:

- Do I still have buyer's remorse?
- Do I make a purchase knowing it is not a good idea?
- What percentage of times do I second guess myself?
- Am I in control of my money?

As you build your self trust by validating your accomplishments, you are ready to put past mistakes to rest. At the same time you will be putting an unconscious fear of repeating past financial mistakes to rest as well as the associated internal critic chatter. One way to break through this fear is to learn the wisdom contained in what you have named a mistake, to forgive yourself, and to make different choices in the future.

~~~~~~~~~~~~~~

Wallet Wisdom Lesson

Change one thing
and you change your world.

~~~~~~~~~~~~~~

Chapter

7 Get Back on Track

I agree to take appropriate action when breaking these agreements.

The preceding agreements have challenged you to think about how negative money behaviors limit your ability to generate wealth and wisdom. While the Action Items that accompany each agreement are designed to engage you in taking a specific action, the purpose of this final agreement is to create a systematic approach to taking appropriate action. This agreement completes the three-part *Wealth and Wisdom System* as it incorporates the other six agreements. The first six agreements have served to change the way you think about money, help you become more proactive, and put the past to rest. This agreement puts your new way of thinking into motion.

The Wealth and Wisdom System

Your current money situation may be muddy and filled with emotional clutter, unresolved past issues and negative beliefs. Your **INTENTIONS** are wealth building blocks. The **AGREEMENTS** are the consciousness that keeps you on track and solid, while the old outdated beliefs about money disappear. **ACTION STEPS** put it all together.

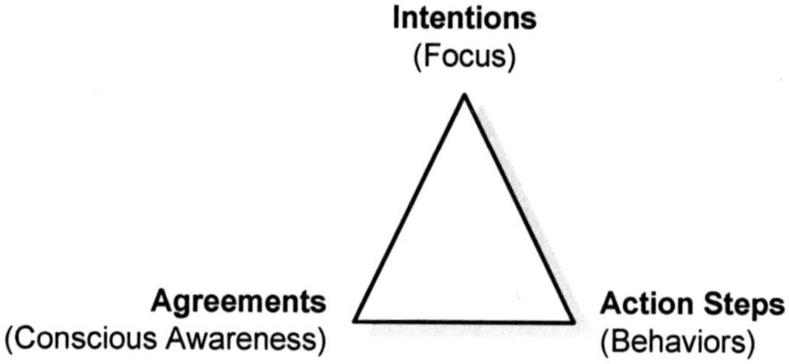

Focus + Conscious Awareness + Behavior

=

Wealth and Wisdom

Intentions and Goals

In any number of situations, it is easier to take the appropriate action when you have clearly defined intentions. Though the clarifying intention may share similarities with setting goals, your intentions delve even deeper into your emotional payoffs. A goal is typically tied to a time frame and specific numbers, such as saving $1,000 by Christmas or earning $10,000 by the end of the month. Your intention is the *goal of the goal*, or the real *result of the result* you desire, rather than only the money. It is the quality of emotional life you wish to achieve as a result from achieving the monetary goal. An intention puts that quality into motion as if you had already attained the particular money goal.

Our culture teaches that you must have goals to accomplish success. Nothing could be further from the truth for the vast majority of people. Setting goals and then not achieving them in the set amount of time is self-defeating. Even when goals are achieved, there are many people who experience an internal sense of emptiness. There is a tendency to second guess with negative, nasty critic self-talk that says things like, “The goal should have been higher” or “Think of how much better you could have done if the goals were even more difficult to achieve.”

Goals, by themselves, set up a self-perpetuating cycle of "never enough," no matter how much you achieve.

George, a commissioned salesman, came to understand how his goals were setting him up for failure. George a set a monthly income goal of $25,000, and found that he often fell short—one month he made $23,457, the next month he made $24,890, and the following month sales dropped to $19,456. He felt understandably frustrated because he focused entirely on the fact that he wasn't meeting the $25,000 mark. George used the missed number to prove to himself that he was a failure over and over again. He was beginning to give up on himself by making an internal decision that somehow he was defective or lacked skills or was just a victim of bad luck. But what if George could move past the magic dollar amount he had in mind and think about why a $25,000 income stream each month is important?

George was asked to imagine what would change (in his life) if he had consistently achieved his $25,000 goal. Upon reflection, he said that by earning the $25,000, he would feel relaxed, stable, and confident. The number $25,000 represented relaxation, stability, and confidence to George. Once George recognized the real intention, he was no longer bound by the numbers. His intention opened up his mind to the possibility of considering himself successful earning more than $25,000 each month, or less, all the while focusing on attaining the relaxation, stability, and confidence he desired. He is more likely to attain his numbered goals and beyond because he is focused on a certain state of mind. rather than on a specific number. This intention gave him focus and direction to his action steps. As a result, he now engages only in those activities that align with his intention. These may include getting some exercise, reading a new sales book, or contacting some of his existing clients to see if they have additional projects. The next action step to take comes more naturally as George reviews his commitment to be relaxed, stable, and confident. Any activity that brings him stress or saps his energy in any way will be considered the opposite of his intention or a breakdown.

Goals leave out a significant missing piece of wealth-building, but goal setting has been so deeply ingrained that it is often difficult to get underneath the goal to the real intention. Like George, Janet initially was not able to separate her goal from her intention. She thought she simply wanted to be a better money manager and get her clutter organized. She complained about her files being a mess and how she could never find what she needed; yet she somehow never found the time to straighten out the mess. The task became a burden that constantly hung over her head. Instead of ruminating over the lack of organization, Janet needed to dig deeper to the real cause of her frustration—understanding that getting organized was simply an action step, not a result.

Janet needed to focus on the core benefit of managing her money and being well organized. By separating her goal from her intention, she realized that she wanted to "be secure and stable with her money." Getting her files and receipts organized was her first action step. Until these intended results were clarified, Janet was running around in circles trying too hard to get organized. Once she saw that being organized was simply an action step on the path to wealth and wisdom, she hired a professional organizer to work with her to cut through the clutter.

Janet found that she did not necessarily need to have the perfect filing system. Instead, she began building a track record of financial successes by staying focused on her intention. You may or may not have intentions similar to George and Janet, but no matter what you desire, you can accomplish it easier by focusing on the qualities of life that are important to you. Once you do this, taking appropriate actions toward being wealthy is more natural. Much like an umbrella over money goals, your intention is the core benefit to be received once the goal is accomplished.

~~~~~~~~~~~~~

Wallet Wisdom Lesson

An intention without action
is just a
good idea.

~~~~~~~~~~~~~

An intention is a statement of how you want to be, written as if you already are. Your intention is the result of bridging the gap between where you are and where you want to be. Your intention statement does not put any stipulations or conditions on your achievement, nor does it restrict action steps by demanding that you accomplish it in a certain way. The intention works with your heart's desire—clearing the way in a manner that may not make sense to you.

~~~~~~~~~~~~~

Wallet Wisdom Lesson

Scattered energy
blocks money.
Focused energy attracts it.

~~~~~~~~~~~~~

As you write your intention in your own hand, you may already sense what action to take, but that action itself is not actually stated in the intention. Do any of these statements fit with your money intentions?

- Be financially joyous and at ease with myself.
- Be focused, consistent, and financially stable.
- Be peaceful and relaxed with my money.
- Be secure within myself.
- Be stable and confident with money.
- Be in a harmonious money partnership with my spouse/significant other.
- Be respectful of myself and my money.
- Be financially confident, safe, and secure.
- Be peaceful and at ease with my newfound wealth.
- Be financially powerful and energized.
- Be consistent, relaxed, and financially at peace.
- Be energized, relaxed, and financially flourishing.

Because the purpose of identifying your intention is to bring focus, clarity, and direction to your activities, you will not want to have more than one at a time. You will know when you are ready to move on to a new intention by observing the results of your original intention in your life. The order of the words will tell you what is most important to you and where your energy will go first. Avoid intentions that have more than three cohesive qualities of life, as that may scatter energy instead of giving focus to your journey. You can use the words below in an intention statement that starts with the word "BE," avoiding the word "to" in your intention statement, because it keeps the intention always in the future.

consistent	accepting	comfortable	calm
dignified	honest	cooperative	happy
confident	relaxed	harmonious	peaceful
free	safe	energetic	committed
rational	stable	composed	trusting

My intention is ______________________________

By writing down your intention in your own handwriting, you have set a powerful energy into motion whether you are conscious of it or not. You will start to see how daily events relate to your intentions as either breakdowns or breakthroughs as you relate these daily events to your intention. It is in the nature of this intentional energy that you may have what is defined, for our purposes, as breakdowns; the bright side is that you will be able to convert any real or imagined break*downs* into break-*throughs* quickly by using the agreements as consciousness guide-posts.

Breakdowns are events that seem like barriers to your intentions. Let's say you have the intended result of "being fulfilled and comfortable with money." A breakdown might be a minor roof repair that you've put off for a long time, so long that it eventually becomes a major repair you can no longer ignore. This situation would probably produce anxiety instead of the comfort you desire. A breakdown such as this should signal you to stop, take a deep breath, and review the rest of the agreements. Have you been telling yourself the truth about the seriousness of needing to repair the roof? Did you spend money on unnecessary items without thinking about the roof repairs? Have you been worrying about the roof instead of taking action? The rest of the agreements will tell you what immediate action to take in the future so you do not repeat the behavior that caused the breakdown.

The opposite of a breakdown is a breakthrough. Breakthroughs are events that spur behavior changes, give you insights, and bring you closer to your intended results. Using the same intended result of "being fulfilled and comfortable with money," a breakthrough would be researching and finding a trustworthy roofer who charges a reasonable price, or it could be receiving an unexpected bonus at work that more than pays for your roof repairs. Again, look at which of the agreements are in motion and have allowed you to accept the extra money with a gracious gratitude.

There may be times when you forget about the agreements or are too embroiled in difficult circumstances to even think about them. This is the time to stop the roller-coaster drama for a few quiet moments, slow down, breathe, and notice if you are having more breakdowns than breakthroughs. If this is the case, it is easy to get back on track by reviewing the agreements. Which one seems to cause the most difficulty? That is the one to focus on taking appropriate action or perhaps completing one of the Action Items at the end of the chapter. It is a great practice to stay on track with the agreements by setting time aside to do a weekly review of your intentions similar to the format below. On a sheet of paper, list your breakthroughs and breakdowns, using your intention as the benchmark. Remember that the breakdowns and breakthroughs both are associated with your intention, so you may want to write the intention at the top of the page. It may look something like this:

My intention is ______________________________

Breakdowns	**Breakthroughs**

Converting Breakdowns to Breakthroughs

The second part of the *Wealth and Wisdom System* is the agreements. These agreements are the conscious awareness that supports you achieving not only wealth, but wisdom. All three parts of the *Wealth and Wisdom System* are connected, including the breakdowns and breakthroughs. Sometimes the same breakdown may be related to more than one of the agreements, although in some rare instances, you will not see an immediate connection to any of the agreements. If this should happen, review your intention. If you do not have a clear, focused intention, your breakdowns and breakthroughs may seem random and beyond your control. This is just another sneaky way for your mind to keep you stuck in your current thinking, so be vigilant if there appears to be no connection.

Rating the Agreements

After you write down your breakdowns and breakthroughs, rate how well you've kept the agreements on a scale of 1-10, with 10 being the highest rating.

____ Stop complaining, blaming, and worrying about money.

____ Be creative, open, and flexible to generating and receiving money.

____ Be current and complete on all financial transactions.

____ Think before I buy or do not spend at all.

____ Communicate openly and honestly with myself and others.

____ Trust myself to make reasonable and rational financial decisions.

____ Take appropriate action when breaking these agreements.

Now that you have rated the agreements, the next step is to connect the breakdowns and breakthroughs to your ratings. For example, a sudden need for the major car repair may seem like it "just happened", but upon closer examination, you may find that you have not been telling yourself the truth about the car needing maintenance. More often than not, breakdowns are connected to one or more of the lowest rated agreements. The amount of time you stay in breakdown will be considerably shorter when you can connect the breakdown to the agreement and then take appropriate action.

If you had a breakdown by unconsciously spending, then you would take action to raise your rating of agreement #5, *Think before I buy or do not spend at all*. An Action Item to counteract this breakdown might be writing down everything you spend each day in order to be conscious of your spending habits. Practice making a connection between breakdowns and breakthroughs and how you rated the Agreements. By practicing the connection, you will become better at gauging the appropriate action to take. Taking action is what converts breakdowns into breakthroughs.

Breakdown ________________ Agreement ________________

Breakdown ________________ Agreement ________________

Breakdown ________________ Agreement ________________

Breakdown ________________ Agreement ________________

Review your breakthroughs. Most likely you will find that your breakthroughs are related to rating one or more of the agreements between 7 and 10. The higher you rate the agreements, the more breakthroughs you will have while walking the road to wealth.

Breakthrough ________________ Agreement ________________

Breakthrough ________________ Agreement ________________

Breakthrough ________________ Agreement ________________

Breakthrough ________________ Agreement ________________

It may initially seem like the action steps you take are not important because they feel small or insignificant, but wealth is driven by commitment to action that demonstrates your commitment to breakthrough. Sometimes you may not know what actions steps to take or you may feel afraid to venture into a new way of doing things until you are certain of the outcome. The importance of the action step is the symbolic nature of making a commitment to change. It matters little if the action step makes sense in the moment you are doing it.

For example, writing down what you are spending may not seem like it will make a difference in your spending habits. However, until you do it, you will never know if being more aware of what you are doing will change your spending behavior. Begin where you are and pretend you are like a baby taking your first wobbling steps on the journey to a flourishing, vibrantly, wealthy life. Like a baby taking its first steps, when you fall down, get back up and take corrective action instead of dwelling on what went wrong. Change your pattern by doing something different, even if it doesn't make sense at the time. Take a breakthrough action step as if you were an emboldened child. While a particular action step does not guarantee it will produce the intended result, it does produce positive motion towards wealth and wisdom.

Chapter

8 Conclusion: The Journey

You may feel a bit strange or uncomfortable as you take consistent, productive action and begin to see wonderful things coming your way. It is as if you hardly know or recognize yourself. Be assured that when you look in the mirror you will see the same person, but you will have a sense that you are not the same inside. Do not be surprised if there is a strange feeling of uneasiness. You are just getting to know the new, Wealthy U that is emerging from within. Even as you are celebrating your newfound wisdom and wealth, there may be a nagging feeling that this is not real. You may feel like you are standing on sand; the shifting, sandy sensation will change to a solid prosperous grounding as you take continue to take consistent, positive action steps.

As you take these action steps, it is helpful to remember that people tend to be creatures of habit that resist even positive changes. Something as simple as getting a new car with the gas tank on the opposite side as in your old car can cause you to continually be prepared to put gas in the wrong side of the car. Try switching your wristwatch to your other arm for a day or two. You might find yourself looking for your wristwatch in the same place it has always been. Chances are, in a very short time, you will move your watch back to "where it belongs." When changing into the wealthy person you are meant to be, you must change much more than just a wristwatch. In fact, you must change just about everything from the way you view yourself and your behavior to what others may think about you. Even prosperous changes stretch the internal comfort zone.

The internal comfort zone is the place where you feel safe with what you already know and have experienced. Staying in this unconscious comfort zone is one of the many reasons people stop taking effective action. They fear, on some level, that they might actually accomplish what they want. People do not consciously know they may actually fear having the very thing for which they strive, but just when they are on the cusp of prosperous living, they will give up or string together a set of excuses that seem very real to them.

Wealthy U does not need to be one of these people. You are ready to accept the path to wealth and wisdom by answering, "Yes, I am ready to give up, for all time, the 'poor me' talk." Look into your heart and answer honestly. Would you rather tell a new tale about how you are achieving wealth and wisdom than the same old story of frustration and despair? Before you answer, pause to remember that financial drama has been part of your life for a long time. Are you ready to divorce this dialog forever and step into a new you without ruminating on the past? Your new conversation is about the exciting action steps you are taking towards your vision, dreams, purpose, and your wealth and wisdom.

If you are truly ready, make sure to take the action steps recommended in each chapter and write down your dreams and visions, giving yourself a roadmap to achieving the rich, fulfilled life you desire. Then stay on track with these lessons and enjoy being wealthy. Stay conscious of your money behaviors and continue taking productive action steps each day. Be sure to take time to consider the following questions:

1. **Have a higher cause?**
   Is there a bigger reason to get up in the morning other than just making it through the day? Revisit your vision statement and look closely at your definition of success. Write down your reasons for what you are doing and put it where you will see it each day.

2. **Cut your ties to the past?**
   You will not get to second base by keeping one foot on first. Continue to forgive yourself for past mistakes.

3. **Muster the innate ability to manage your behavior on a daily basis?**
   Nothing happens without you putting action behind your intentions. Make a commitment to a self-management system that works for you. Keep a victory log of daily wins to build self-trust.

4. **Keep a prosperity journal?**
   A journal relieves the mind of the daily clutter we collect. It is a great place to dump your internal critic. Your journal will help you eliminate complaining, blaming, and worry.

5. **Money is nothing more than an exchange of value.**
   Value given for value received. Because this is so, it logically follows that the ultimate value is valuing yourself. There is a direct connection between inner worth and outer wealth. How much money a person has or does not have and the spirit with which they use and steward that money is a reflection of how they view themselves. Make it a practice to recognize your personal value as a unique human being. Wealth opens up more choices to celebrate your successes and accomplishments. It allows you to you give to yourself and to give of yourself back to the world. Your quest for wealth and wisdom proves that you are an amazing person who takes seriously the ideal of living a rich, full life. Yet, right now you are more valuable than any amount of money you will ever attain.

As you see the evidence of wealth and wisdom in your life, you will have simply achieved the next stage in your journey. As long as you are alive and vibrantly seeking, you will naturally begin the journey to wealth and wisdom again and again, constantly rewriting a new, more powerful vision for the life you desire. The wealth and wisdom pathway offers no endings, only new beginnings.

May you always enjoy being Wealthy U.

About the Author

Marilyn August

Marilyn August is a Business Advisor, Wealth Coach, and founder of Wealth & Wisdom Seminars (http://wealthyu.com), a company devoted to increasing productivity by changing the way people think about money.

Ms. August advises business owners and commissioned sales professionals for the purposes of increasing their profitable productivity using the powerful tools and techniques she developed over the past two decades.

She is a popular speaker on the topic, "Mind Over Money," and has hosted her own radio show, "The Money Game."

Ms. August has been a Business Consultant for the Small Business Development Center in Santa Ana, California (SBA), where she excelled at developing and implementing strategic business plans. Marilyn has been featured in the *Los Angeles Times* and the *Orange County Register newspapers,* as well as *OC Metro Magazine*. Marilyn's professional background also includes over ten years as a corporate trainer for international companies such as American Honda Corporation, AAA, and the Chicago Motor Club. Ms. August holds a Masters Degree from Northern Illinois University, DeKalb, Illinois.

Submit your prosperity success stories to Marilyn@wealthyu.com. Be sure to include mention of which one of the Seven Sacred Wealth & Wisdom Lessons helped you to break through. Selected stories will be posted on her Web site and credited to you along with a gift certificate for a complimentary consultation and FREE book sent to a person of your choice.

Remember to take advantage of the two FREE BOOK BONUSES.

Two FREE BOOK BONUSES are available to you right now as a gift for being on the Journey to Wealth & Wisdom.

The Wealth & Wisdom Tracking Sheet gives you an alternative to budgets. Instructions for using the tracking sheet can be found on the Wealthy U Web site (http://wealthyu.com).

Wallet Wisdom Lessons are given throughout this book and are downloadable at the Wealthy U Web site in a format suitable for framing.

Sign up for the Wallet Wisdom monthly newsletter at
http://wealthyu.com

Books

Other Happy About® Books

Purchase these books at Happy About http://happyabout.info or at other online and physical bookstores.

Networking Online—Making LinkedIn Work for you!

This book explains the benefits of using LinkedIn and recommends best practices so that you can get the most out of it.

Paperback: $19.95
eBook: $11.95

Is it who or what one knows that makes the difference? Both!

Get the you tips, techniques and shares anecdotal stories that will help you succeed with your networking goals.

Paperback $19.95
eBook $11.95

CPSIA information can be obtained at www.ICGtesting.com
Printed in the USA
LVOW12s2044280713

345008LV00001B/21/P

9 781600 050992